do it **NOW** *do it* FAST *do it* **RIGHT**™

Lighting

Solutions

Lighting solutions.

OFFICIALLY WITHDRAWN

do it **NOW** *do it* **FAST** *do it* **RIGHT**™

Lighting
Solutions

The Taunton Press

The Taunton Press
Inspiration for hands-on living®

The Taunton Press, Inc., 63 South Main Street, PO Box 5506, Newtown, CT 06470-5506

e-mail: tp@taunton.com

Distributed by Publishers Group West

WRITER AND PROJECT MANAGER: Joseph Truini

SERIES EDITOR: Tim Snyder

SERIES DESIGN: Lori Wendin

LAYOUT: Cathy Cassidy

ILLUSTRATOR: Melanie Powell

COVER PHOTOGRAPHERS: (front cover) all photos © Geoffrey Gross, except main photo ©Randy O'Rourke;

(back cover) all photos © Geoffrey Gross, except bottom row far left and far right © Randy O'Rourke

Taunton's Do It Now/Do It Fast/Do It Right™ is a trademark of
The Taunton Press, Inc., registered in the U.S. Patent and Trademark Office.

Library of Congress Cataloging-in-Publication Data
Lighting solutions.
      p. cm. -- (Do it now/do it fast/do it right)
   ISBN 1-56158-669-2
   1. Lighting. 2. Electric lighting. I. Series.
   TH7703.L56 2004
   747'.92--dc22

                              2004001355

Printed in the United States of America
10 9 8 7 6 5 4 3 2 1

The following manufacturers/names appearing in Lighting Solutions are trademarks: AOSafety®; Black & Decker®;
Bucket Boss®; CoolMax™; Crescent®; Fat Max™; Husky®; Ideal Industries®; Irwin™; The Pocket Pal®; Reflex™;
Romex®; Stanley®; Wire-Nut®.

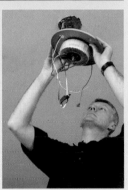

Acknowledgments

We're grateful to the lighting manufacturers and their representatives who contributed photographs and products shown on these pages, including: Phil Kinzer (Intermatic), Joann Wills (Seagull Lighting), Marilyn Elam (Hunter-Kenroy), Carl Cohen (Juno Lighting), Gina Rueff (Thomas Lighting), and Ansley Welchel (Progress Lighting). Thanks to Kathy Ziprik (Style Solutions) for helping to procure the decorative ceiling medallions. Thanks also to electrician Peter Eng of Electrical Enterprises for lending his considerable skills and talents to this book.

Contents

LIGHTING PROJECTS

Elegant Entry 22

Brighten up your front entry with a
light that offers SECURITY & STYLE

Bath Vanity Revival 36

Brighten the bathroom view with
a MULTILIGHT fixture that's easy to
install

Recessed Light Retrofit 48

Tired of that old ceiling light?
Achieve a LOW-PROFILE, HIGH-
STYLE solution with a "can" light
that's easy to customize

How to Use This Book

I F YOU'RE INTERESTED IN HOME IMPROVEMENTS that add value and convenience while also enabling you to express your own sense of style, you've come to the right place. **Do It Now/ Do It Fast/Do It Right** books are created with an attitude that says "Let's get started!" and an ideal mix of home improvement inspiration and how-to information. Do it Now books don't skip important steps or force you to guess at what needs to be done to take a project from start to finish.

You'll find that this book has a friendly, easy-to-use format. (See the sample pages opposite.) You'll begin each project knowing exactly what tools and gear you'll need, and what materials to buy at your home center or building supply outlet. You can get started confidently because every step is illustrated and explained. Along the way, you'll discover plenty of expert advice packed into the margins. For ideas on how to personalize your project, check out the design options pages that follow the step-by-step instructions.

WORK TOGETHER

If you like company when you go to the movies or clean up the kitchen, you'll probably feel the same way about tackling home improvement projects. The work will go faster, and you'll have a partner to share in the adventure. You'll

Get the TOOLS & GEAR you need. You'll also find out what features and details are important.

DO IT NOW helps to keep your project on track with timely advice.

LINGO explains words that the pros know.

WHAT CAN GO WRONG explains how to avoid common mistakes.

SHOPPING TIPS offer hints on buying your materials.

COOL TOOL puts you in touch with tools that make the job easier.

see that some projects really call for another set of hands to steady a ladder or keep the project going smoothly. Read through the project you'd like to tackle and note where you're most likely to need help.

PLANNING AND PRACTICE PAY OFF

Most of the projects in this book can easily be completed in a weekend. But the job can take longer if you don't pay attention to planning and project preparation requirements. Check out the conditions in the area where you'll be working. Sometimes repairs are required before you can begin your project. For help, check out the basic techniques in Prep Projects (p. 14). Get Set (p. 4) will tell you about the tools and materials required for most of the projects in this book.

Your skill and confidence will improve with every project you complete. But if you're trying a technique for the first time, it's wise to rehearse before you "go live." This means ordering a little extra in the way of supplies and materials, and finding a location where you can practice your technique.

DESIGN OPTIONS Complete your project with different dimensions, finishes, and details. Explore design options to personalize your project.

DO IT FAST! saves you time and trouble.

WHAT CAN GO WRONG explains how to avoid common mistakes.

STEP BY STEP Get started, keep going and finish the job. Every step is illustrated and explained.

Get Set

New lighting begins with a **QUICK GUIDE** to terminology, tools, & supplies

O NE OF THE EASIEST and most effective ways to enhance the look and livability of your home is to replace old, out-dated lights with new fixtures. New light fixtures can enliven dreary rooms, make small spaces seem bigger, add curb appeal, accent special artwork, and express a new sense of style. Better lighting also means a safer home environment. And unlike many other home-improvement upgrades,

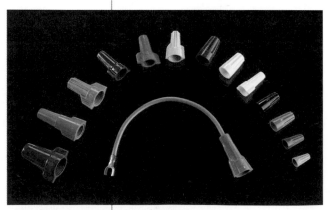

installing new lights doesn't require a large investment in time or tools. But before attempting any lighting project, you'll need a basic understanding of the various types of lighting used in a home, the safety procedures you need to follow, and the tools and supplies you'll need.

▶ DO IT RIGHT

When installing task lighting, position each fixture to eliminate glare off shiny surfaces. Also, be sure that you won't block the light when standing or sitting in the work area.

✓ UPGRADE

Replace a standard rectangular fluorescent light with an attractive "cloud" fixture. Its rounded, softer design is much more appealing. This particular model hangs 1 in. down from the ceiling, which creates a pleasing halo effect.

▌ LINGO

If you're paging through a lighting catalog, you'll find that some manufacturers refer to ambient lighting as general lighting.

Different Types of Lighting

Whether you're looking at the lights in your house or making your way through the dazzling display of lighting fixtures at your local home center, you'll be glad to know that this universe divides pretty easily into three lighting categories: ambient, task, and accent. As you begin to upgrade the light fixtures in your home, keep in mind that a well-designed lighting scheme incorporates all three types of lighting.

AMBIENT LIGHTING provides the primary illumination for a room, and it's usually the first light that you turn on. Ambient lighting is typically provided by a centrally located ceiling fixture or a few strategically placed fixtures. However, it can also be provided by table lamps or a ceiling fan that includes a light. During the day, ambient light enters the room through windows, exterior doors, and skylights.

In this well-lit kitchen, indirect ambient light is provided by fixtures mounted above the cabinets. Under-cabinet lights and a pair of hanging lamps provide task lighting.

In a bathroom, task lighting must be functional and beautiful. The light-toned walls in this bathroom reflect a good amount of light, enabling a pair of small fixtures to provide ample illumination.

These recessed fixtures are fitted with adjustable eyeballs to direct accent light toward the fireplace mantel.

TASK LIGHTING, as its name suggests, provides sufficient light for specific "work" activities, such as chopping vegetables, reading, or folding laundry. Unlike ambient lighting, task lighting should deliver light to a specific area. In a kitchen, the most common type of task lighting is under-cabinet lighting. But a ceiling-mounted light, located above a kitchen island or table, can provide both ambient and task light. The same is true for track lighting.

ACCENT LIGHTING is the most dramatic type of light and is primarily used to set the mood of a room. For mood control, wire task light fixtures to dimmer switches. Accent lighting is also commonly used to illuminate paintings, art objects, and other items displayed on walls and shelves. Accent lighting can be provided by wall-mounted sconces, track lights, or recessed fixtures fitted with eyeball or spotlight trim kits.

Working Safely with Electricity

A little bit of anxiety about making electrical connections is a good thing. But don't let that stop you from taking on lighting projects. You can handle any of the projects in this book, and many others, if you follow the safety precautions explained below.

1 Turn off the electricity before starting any electrical project. Always shut off the power to the circuit you're working on. Do this at the main electrical panel, which is typically located in the basement, crawl space, garage, or utility closet.

2 Wear safety goggles and a dust mask when removing old fixtures, drilling holes, and cutting through walls and ceilings.

3 Read and follow the installation instructions that come with a new light fixture.

4 Replace or reattach any ceiling box that has come loose; never hang a light fixture from a wobbly box.

There's a wide range of safety glasses available, including ones with tinted lenses. For optimum protection, choose full-coverage goggles or a model with side shields.

Safety first: Go to the main electrical panel and turn off the power to the circuit you'll be working on. Most panels have circuit breakers, as shown here.

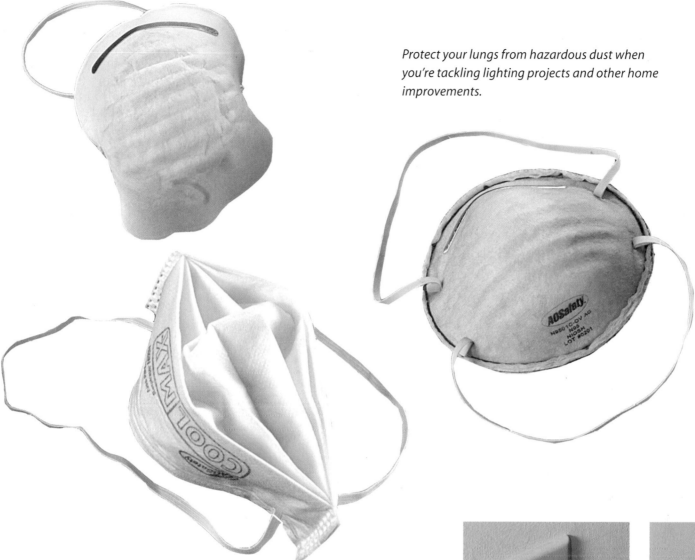

Protect your lungs from hazardous dust when you're tackling lighting projects and other home improvements.

5⏐ Be sure that every cable that enters a metal box is held in place by a cable connector that's secured to the box.

6⏐ Never hang a ceiling fan from a standard outlet box. Use only a fan-approved box.

7⏐ When cutting into a wall or ceiling, use caution to avoid damaging any hidden pipes or cables.

8⏐ House all wire connections and splices inside an approved, covered electrical box.

9⏐ Don't add lights to an existing circuit without first consulting a licensed electrician. Overloading a circuit can create a potential fire hazard.

10⏐ Get help when you need it. If you encounter a situation that's unfamiliar or confusing, stop and consult a licensed electrician.

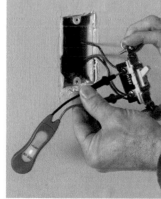

A plug-in circuit analyzer (at left) can quickly tell if an outlet is wired correctly. A series of lights indicate, among other things, if wires are interchanged or not connected. An inexpensive neon tester (at right) can be used to determine if the electrical power is on at switches, outlets, fuses, cords, and motors.

Keep all your electrical tools neatly organized by storing them in their own carrying case or toolbox.

The combination wrench, which has an open end and box end, has been radically redesigned. This much-improved version has a pivoting joint, which allows the box end to work in tight spaces and at awkward angles. It's also equipped with a ratcheting mechanism.

The Basic Toolbox

Lighting projects get done faster and easier when you've got the right tools. If you fill your toolbox with the gear described below, you'll be well equipped to handle any lighting project in this book, plus plenty more. The same tools will also help you with general electrical work around the house.

DRILL & DRIVE TOOLS. A multitip screwdriver will enable you to take on any screw that you encounter in wiring work. The model shown here has seven double-ended bits, so there are 14 different driving tips you can use. Shaped like screwdrivers, nutdrivers are also useful. And don't forget a cordless drill/driver. This portable power tool is equally useful for drilling holes and driving screws. To go with your cordless drill, buy a drill index (a set of twist-type bits) and several spade-type bits (⅜ in., ¾ in., 1 in.). An assortment of screwdriving and nutdriving bits will also be helpful.

PLIERS. Pliers are required for pulling wires, gripping parts, and tightening nuts. To be really well equipped, get linesman, needle-nose, and tongue-and-groove pliers.

WIRE STRIPPER & CABLE RIPPER. The stripper is a plier-shaped tool designed to cut, strip, and bend wire. Buy a combination stripper that

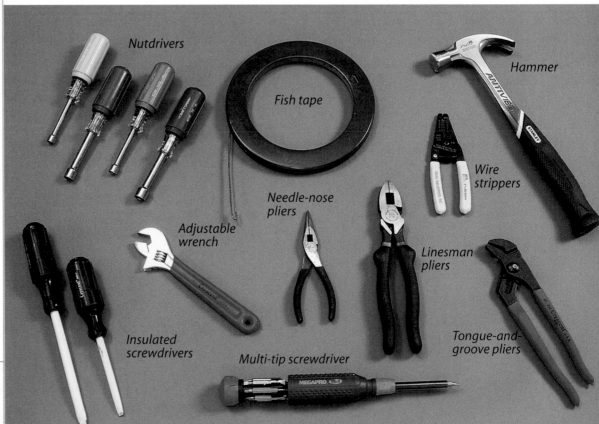

Nutdrivers

Fish tape

Hammer

Wire strippers

Needle-nose pliers

Adjustable wrench

Linesman pliers

Insulated screwdrivers

Tongue-and-groove pliers

Multi-tip screwdriver

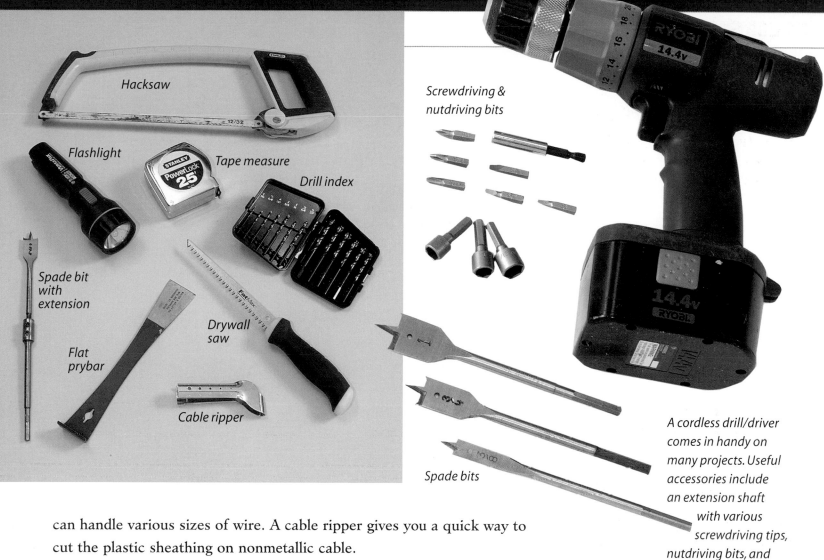

Hacksaw

Flashlight

Tape measure

Drill index

Spade bit with extension

Flat prybar

Drywall saw

Cable ripper

Screwdriving & nutdriving bits

14.4v

Spade bits

A cordless drill/driver comes in handy on many projects. Useful accessories include an extension shaft with various screwdriving tips, nutdriving bits, and assorted spade bits.

can handle various sizes of wire. A cable ripper gives you a quick way to cut the plastic sheathing on nonmetallic cable.

FISH TAPE. Electricians use fish tape to snake wires through walls, across ceilings, or along floors. You can do the same, although you may want to call in a pro for more difficult snaking work. The tape is actually a spool of spring steel that has a hook on one end. You push the narrow tape down a hole until it comes out at the desired location. Then hook your electrical cable to the end of the tape and pull it through.

SAWS. You'll need a hacksaw to cut metal conduit, armored cable, and aluminum track. For cutting through drywall and plaster, get a pointed drywall saw.

FLASHLIGHT. You'll appreciate a light with a strong beam if you need to run wiring in an attic or crawl space.

TAPE MEASURE. A 25-ft. tape will make it easy to measure lengths of cable and chain.

PRYBARS. Available in different sizes, prybars help you to remove old boxes and cable staples. A small-size bar will handle most electrical assignments.

If you're working with a lot of non-metallic cable (Romex®), consider investing in an "NM" wire stripper. It has a specially designed cutter that slices through the outer sheathing without cutting the wires inside.

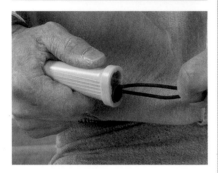

Electrical Supplies

The wide world of electrical upplies can be divided into four basic groups: cable, boxes, connectors, and devices. Now, you won't need all four types for every electrical project, but it's smart to know what's available at your local home center or electrical supplier.

ROMEX & BX CABLE. The cable most commonly used in today's homes is nonmetallic (NM) cable, commonly known as Romex. It consists of three or more wires sheathed in a protective plastic jacket. Your home might also contain some armored cable, known as BX cable. This cable has a flexible steel jacket and is required in some semi-exposed situations, such as when a cable runs through the inside of a cabinet. Check with a licensed electrician for specific questions about whether to use BX or NM cable.

Electrical cable is also described by wire gauge (thickness). For most lighting projects around the house, you'll use 14/2 or 12/2 cable. Cable designated as 14/2 can handle 15 amps; 12/2 cable can handle 20-amp fixtures.

ELECTRICAL BOXES. All electrical connections must take place inside of a metal or plastic electrical box. If you're replacing an old light fixture with a new one, you can usually reuse the electrical box that is already in

Types of Cable

1 14/2 NM cable	5 14/2 BX armored cable
2 12/2 NM cable	6 14-gauge low-voltage cable
3 10/2 NM cable	7 EMT conduit
4 4/3 NM cable	

1   2   3   4   5   6   7

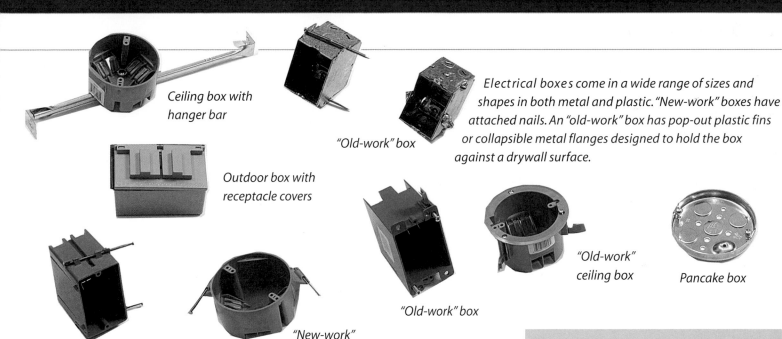

Ceiling box with hanger bar

"Old-work" box

Electrical boxes come in a wide range of sizes and shapes in both metal and plastic. "New-work" boxes have attached nails. An "old-work" box has pop-out plastic fins or collapsible metal flanges designed to hold the box against a drywall surface.

Outdoor box with receptacle covers

"Old-work" ceiling box

Pancake box

"Old-work" box

"New-work" box

"New-work" ceiling box

place. When a new box has to be installed (to install a light, switch, or outlet in a new location), find out what type of box you need by asking a salesperson at your local home center or hardware store. A "new-work" box usually comes with nails attached, so you can nail it to a stud or joist. An "old-work" or "remodel" box has tabs, fins, or clamps designed to help you mount it in existing drywall or plaster.

CONNECTORS. Twist-on connectors, commonly called wire nuts, are used to join together two or more wires. They come in a wide variety of sizes and styles to accommodate most wire gauges. Cable connectors are code-required on metal boxes. They securely hold the cable in place and protect the wires from chafing against the metal box. Plastic boxes have built-in connectors.

A GFCI outlet (shown at right) provides protection against electrical shocks in kitchens, bathrooms, and other damp locations.

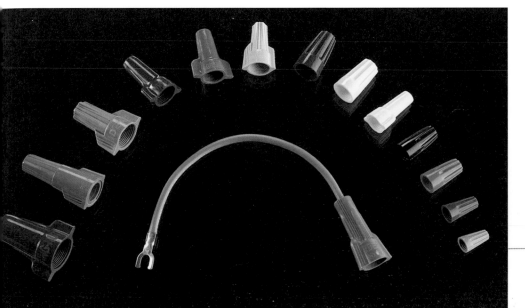

Wire connectors (aka "wire nuts") are used to connect two or more wires. You'll need these twist-on connectors to join the wires on your light fixture to the wires in an electrical box. Be sure to match the size of the connector to the gauge of the wire.

Prep Projects

To get **LIGHTING PROJECTS** done smoothly & safely,
put these tips and techniques to work for you

SWAPPING OUT AN OLD LIGHT FOR A BRAND-NEW FIXTURE can be an uncomplicated job. But there are other times when you'll need to do some extra work to get the job done. That's where a few key techniques and tricks can help out. The prep projects in this chapter will help you add new wiring by tapping into an existing circuit, install new electrical boxes, replace switches, and complete other basic wiring tasks.

ROUTING CABLE

INSTALLING A CEILING BOX

WIRING A SWITCH

SPLICING WIRES

▶ DO IT RIGHT

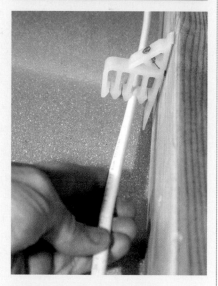

NM (plastic-sheathed) cable should be secured at least every 4½ ft. and within 12 in. of an outlet box, using approved staples or other fasteners. When running multiple cables alongside a stud or ceiling joist, use cable stackers to hold them neatly in place. Each nail-on stacker can hold up to four non-metallic cables.

Routing Cable

1 **BORE A HOLE FOR AN INDICATOR WIRE.** Here's how to connect new electrical cable to an existing circuit without tearing into the wall. After turning off the electricity to the circuit, drill down into your basement or crawl space, using a ¼-in.-dia. bit. Locate your indicator hole up against the wall's shoe molding and directly below the outlet box where your new cable will be connected.

2 **INSERT AN INDICATOR WIRE.** Poke a long "indicator" wire down through the hole. Bend the top end of the wire to prevent it from falling through the floor. Now go into the basement or crawl space and locate the indicator wire.

3 **DRILL UP INTO THE WALL CAVITY.** Measure over from the indicator wire so that you'll be drilling into the wall cavity, directly below the existing outlet box. The distance from your indicator wire depends on the thickness of your wall. If it's a 2x4 wall, you can measure over about 3 in. Bore the hole with a ⅝-in.-dia. spade bit.

4 **PULL THE CABLE INTO THE BOX.** Remove the outlet's cover plate, unscrew the outlet, and pull it out of the box, but don't disconnect any wires. If the outlet box is plastic (as shown here), pry open the clamping fins at the bottom of the box so you can insert your fish tape through a hole in the box. Now "fish" the tape through the access hole you drilled in Step 3. Attach your cable to the end of the fish tape, and pull the cable up into the box. Now you can wire the new cable to the receptacle and extend the cable to your new light fixture or fixture switch.

1

2

3

4

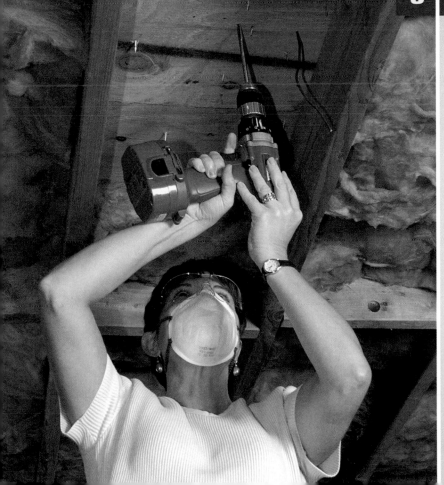

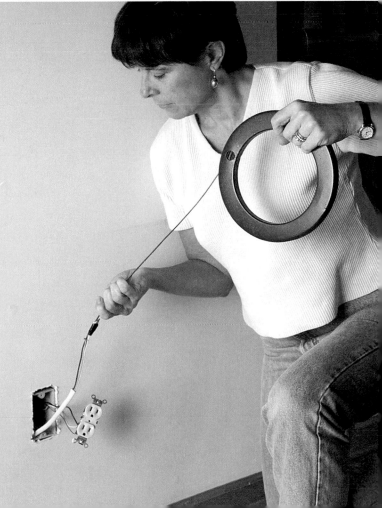

Lighting projects often require you to work in attics and other dark spaces. For safety's sake, use a trouble light that has a fluorescent bulb. It provides more light than an incandescent bulb, uses less electricity, and burns much cooler.

A pancake box (above left) is a shallow box that can be screwed directly to the underside of a joist. A standard box (above right) is deeper and has more room for wire connections, but it must be nailed to the side of a joist.

Adding a Ceiling Box

1 **MOUNT A NEW-WORK BOX.** The method you use to install a ceiling box depends largely on whether or not there's access to the ceiling from above. In new construction or whenever the ceiling joists are exposed, nail a new-work box to a ceiling joist. Simply hold the flat side of the box against the joist and hammer in the nails.

2 **INSTALL A HANGER BAR.** This adjustable bar is what you need if a ceiling light fixture has to be installed exactly in the center of a room. Nail or screw the ends of the metal bar to the joists, then slide the box into position. Tighten the screws inside the box to hold it in place.

3 **ATTACH A WOODEN BRACE.** Here's an alternative to using a hanger bar when the ceiling is accessible from above. Saw a 4-in.-dia. ceiling hole, then cut a 2x4 brace to fit snugly between the joists. Screw a ceiling box to the wooden brace. Set the brace between the joists and secure it by driving 3-in. screws through the joists and into the brace.

4 **USE A FAN BRACE.** When there's no access above the ceiling, install a fan brace. It consists of an adjustable octagonal bar fitted with two metal feet. Each foot is studded with sharp prongs. Cut a 4-in. ceiling hole, then slip the brace through the hole and let the feet rest on the wallboard. Rotate the octagonal bar by hand until you feel the prongs dig into the joists. When you can't hand-tighten any more, use a wrench to rotate the bar one last quarter-turn. Pass the cable through an electrical box, then attach the box with the U-bolt. The fan brace shown can support a 70-lb. ceiling fan or 150-lb. chandelier.

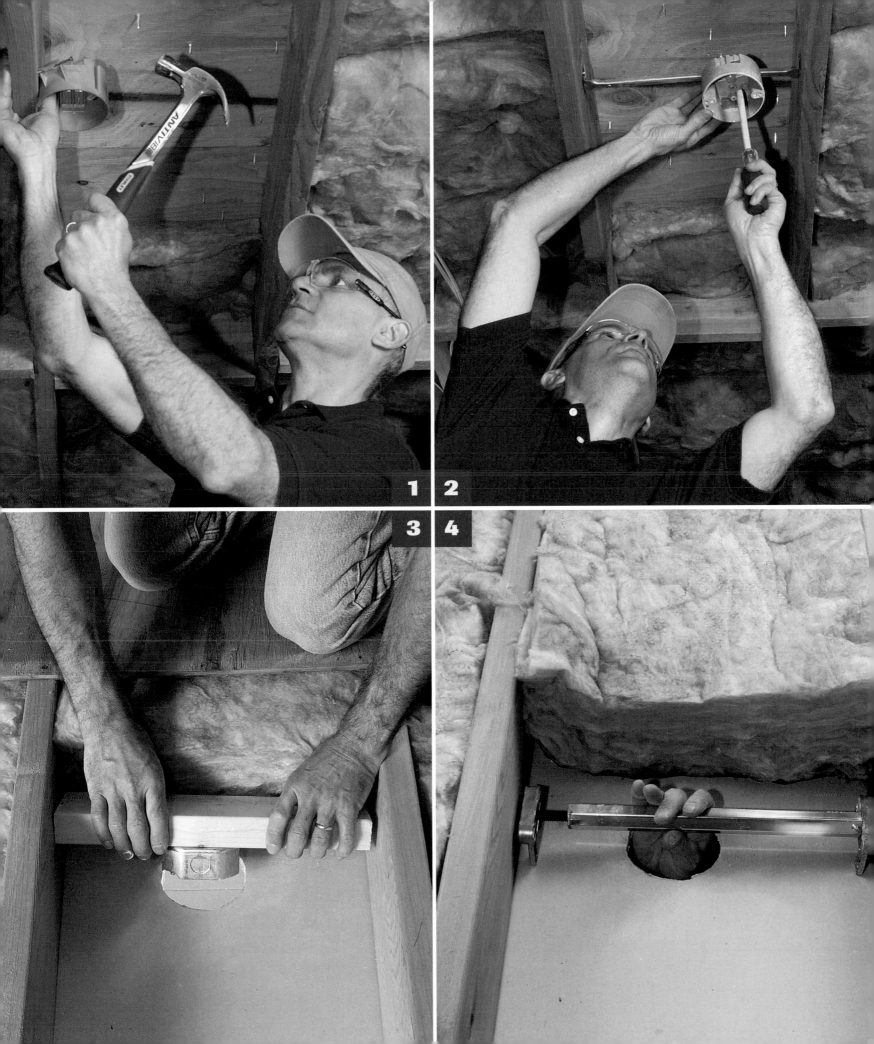

1

2

3

4

Making Wire Connections

1 **CONNECT TO A SCREW TERMINAL.** The preferred way of wiring an outlet or switch is to connect the wires to the screw terminals. Use needle-nose pliers to bend a small hook onto each wire. Slip the wire under the screw head, making sure that it's wrapped clockwise around the screw. That way, the wire will be pulled in as you tighten the screw.

2 **MAKE A PIGTAIL SPLICE.** When there are two or more bare ground wires in a box, cut the wires so that one is at least 4 in. longer than the others. Twist together the wires to make a pigtail splice, then slip a green wire nut over the long wire, and twist it tight over the pigtail. Attach the long wire to the grounding screw on the device.

3 **HOOK UP A THREE-WAY SWITCH.** A three-way switch allows you to operate a light from two different locations, such as from either end of hallway. It's wired with a three-wire cable, which has a black, white, red, and bare ground wire. Exactly how the switch is wired depends on whether or not the power feed is coming through the switch box or the fixture box. (Check the switch's packaging for a wiring schematic.) The switch shown here is located between the light fixture and the second switch. Therefore, the two red wires are attached to the same side of the switch.

4 **MAKE A SWITCH-OPERABLE OUTLET.** For rooms with table lamps, it's convenient to have the lamps plugged into outlets that are operated by wall switches. This is accomplished by isolating the two halves of the outlet so that one half is "always on" and the other half is switch operated. To separate the outlet halves, break off the small metal tab on the side of the outlet.

1 **2**

3 **4**

Elegant Entry

Brighten up your front entry with a light
that offers **SECURITY & STYLE**

WELCOME FAMILY AND FRIENDS INTO YOUR HOME with an attractive new entryway light fixture. Since this is the first fixture someone sees when they enter your home, it should do more than simply provide light. You'll want this light to add style and personality to your entryway.

Here, we'll show you how to replace an old foyer light with a new mini-chandelier that can either be flush-mounted or suspended on a chain. And since the new fixture connects directly to existing wiring, the upgrade from ordinary to gorgeous is quick and easy.

ASSEMBLING THE FIXTURE   REMOVING THE OLD LIGHT   CONNECTING THE WIRES   HANGING THE FIXTURE

Tools & Gear

❋ DO IT NOW

Most light fixtures come with a bag of small parts, fasteners, and pieces of hardware. Keep track of these easy-to-lose items by immediately separating them into two or three food-storage containers. Snap on the lids to keep the parts from spilling out.

❋ DO IT FAST!

Wear clean cotton gloves when removing the light fixture from its original packaging. That will eliminate smudge prints on the finished surfaces and protect you from any sharp edges or glass that may have broken during shipping.

One great thing about do-it-yourself lighting projects is that you don't need a whole garage full of tools. In fact, for most installations you'll only need a few basic hand tools and occasionally an electric drill. Here are the tools used to install the minichandelier:

ADJUSTABLE WRENCH. An indispensable tool for loosening and tightening various hex- and square-head nuts and bolts. To adjust its movable jaw, simply rotate the knurled thumb wheel. Get both an 8-in. and 10-in. wrench and you'll be able to work on virtually any light fixture. For additional comfort, look for ones that have rubber-dipped handles.

DIAGONAL CUTTERS. Sometimes called wire snips, these pointed pliers offer an effortless way to cut wire, cable, string, and even nails. Plus, they're much safer than a utility knife for cutting wire.

SCREWDRIVERS. Your toolbox should include at least two different sizes of Phillips screwdrivers (No. 1 and No. 2) and three slotted screwdrivers ($3/16$-, $1/4$-, $5/16$-in.-wide tips). It's usually more economical to buy screwdrivers in prepackaged sets.

NUTDRIVERS. These useful tools resemble screwdrivers, but work like wrenches. They're ideal for removing hex-head nuts and bolts from deep inside electrical boxes, ceiling cutouts, and other places wrenches won't work. Nut drivers are typically sold in sets that include sizes from $3/16$ in. to $1/2$ in.

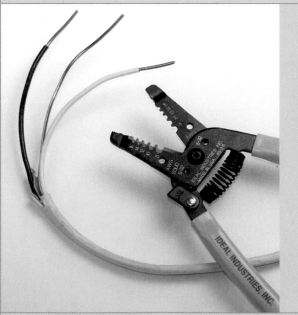

COOL TOOL

A **wire stripper can save you time**, and trouble on many new wiring projects. This plier-like tool is used primarily to remove (strip) plastic insulation from wire, but that's only part of what it can do. Depending on the model, wire strippers also cut and bend wire, crimp insulated terminals and cable connectors, cut machine screws, repair damaged screw threads, and grip like pliers.

Shopping Tips

If you've ever visited a lighting showroom, you know that light fixtures come in a dizzying array of sizes, styles, shapes, and colors. And all those choices make it difficult to find the right fixture. Here are a few tips to use when shopping for an entryway light:

1 Before heading out to a lighting showroom or home center, measure the ceiling height in the foyer. If it's a standard 8-ft.-high ceiling, you'll need a fixture that's no more than 14 in. tall; a taller fixture will hang too low.

2 If you don't see anything you like after a few minutes of shopping, ask the salesperson to show you some lighting catalogs. Each one will have photos of several hundred fixtures, but you can quickly narrow your search to a few dozen by flipping to the "Hallway and Foyer" section.

3 Consult the specifications listed beside each photo. There, you'll find the overall dimensions and finishes available for each fixture. Jot down the model number of any fixture that you like.

4 Many hallway fixtures, including the mini-chandelier we installed (shown below), can be hung from a chain or flush-mounted against the ceiling. That design flexibility allows the fixture to be installed in any foyer, regardless of ceiling height. These fixtures come with about 10 ft. of wire, but only about 2 ft. of chain. If necessary, order more chain from the manufacturer.

COMPONENTS & CONNECTIONS

The drawing shows a flush-mount installation. For ceilings higher than 8 ft. you can suspend this fixture on a chain.

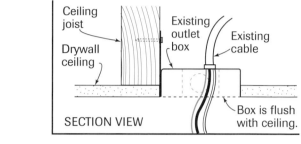

Ceiling joist
Existing outlet box
Existing cable
Drywall ceiling
Box is flush with ceiling.
SECTION VIEW

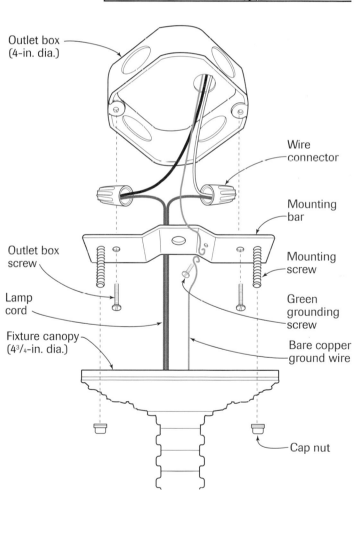

Outlet box (4-in. dia.)
Wire connector
Mounting bar
Outlet box screw
Mounting screw
Lamp cord
Green grounding screw
Fixture canopy ($4^3/_4$-in. dia.)
Bare copper ground wire
Cap nut

Create a staging area for tools and materials by setting up a card table in the room where you'll be working. Cover the table with a canvas drop cloth and then neatly lay out the new fixture, along with all the necessary tools, supplies, and instructions sheet.

After removing the chandelier from its cardboard box, take a close look at the "candles." They often get bent out of place during shipping. To straighten one out, first slip off the hollow candle sleeve from the socket stem and then gently push the metal stem back to a vertical position.

Assembling the New Fixture

1 **THREAD THE COLUMN ONTO THE BASE.** Begin by attaching the base of the fixture (the part with the three candle arms) to the vertical column. Feed the wires coming from the base through the hollow column. Then carefully thread the column onto the base, making sure you don't cross the threads. Use diagonal cutters to trim the wire to length; leave about 12 in. of wire protruding from the top of the column.

2 **UNSCREW THE CHAIN LOOP.** To convert this hanging fixture to a flush-mounted one, you must first remove the chain loop from the top of the column. Grab the steel loop and turn it counterclockwise to unscrew it from the column. Then, use an adjustable wrench to

remove the hex nut that's holding the canopy (the circular plate) onto the end of the column.

3 **REMOVE THE SMALL CANOPY.** Slide the small canopy off the column and replace it with the larger one provided. This switch is necessary because the small canopy isn't big enough to cover the 4-in.-dia. electrical outlet box in the ceiling.

4 **INSTALL THE LARGE CANOPY.** Feed the fixture's wires through the center hole in the larger canopy. Slide the canopy down onto the top of the column and secure it with the hex nut you removed earlier. Now, before proceeding any further, go to the main electrical panel and turn off the power to the foyer light fixture.

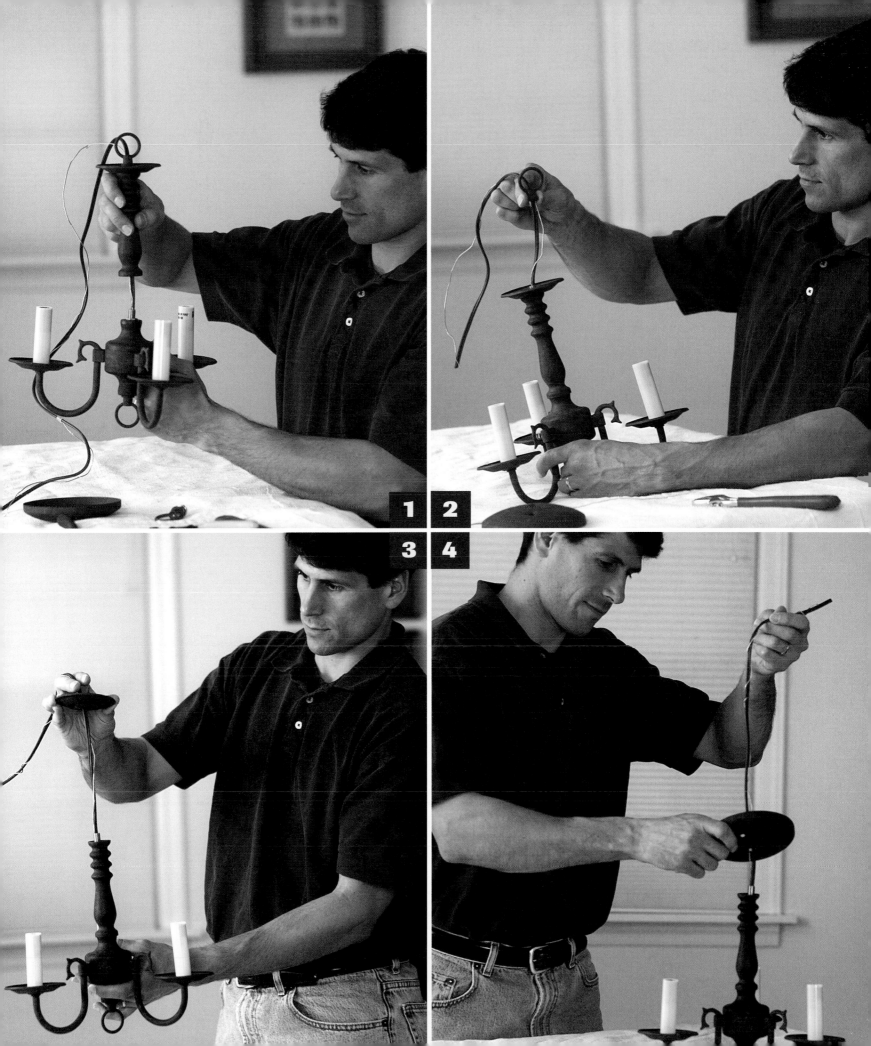

1

2

3

4

▶ **DO IT RIGHT**

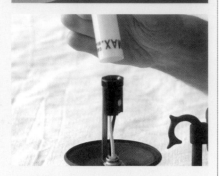

Adhered to one of the candle sleeves is a sticker that tells the maximum wattage bulb you should install in the fixture. That's important information, but the sticker isn't very attractive. Rather than peeling it off, try this: Slip off the sleeve, turn it upside down, and slide it back over the socket stem. Once the chandelier is hung, you won't be able to see the sticker from below. However, it'll always be there to remind you of which size bulbs to use.

:: **DO IT FAST!**

After taking down the old light fixture, you might notice an outline of its base on the ceiling. In some cases, you might have to touch up this discolored area with a fresh coat of paint, but ordinarily you can remove it by lightly rubbing the spot with a damp sponge.

Good-bye Old Light

5 **REMOVE THE GLASS SHADE.** Your old light fixture might be different than the one shown here, but removing it will be similar: Find the screw or knob that holds the glass shade in place and unscrew it by turning it counterclockwise. Keep a firm grip on the shade so it doesn't fall. Then, unscrew the fixture's base from the ceiling by loosening the two mounting screws. In most cases, these screws are tiny balls or knurled knobs that you can twist off by hand.

6 **DISCONNECT THE OLD FIXTURE.** Gently pull the fixture away from the ceiling; watch out for falling dust and debris. Reach up and twist off the plastic connectors (a.k.a.: Wire Nuts) from the ends of the black and white wires. Then, use a screwdriver to disconnect the

bare or green grounding wire, which is secured by a screw to the flat mounting bar or to the outlet box.

7 **UNSCREW THE MOUNTING BAR.** Next, find the flat metal mounting bar that came with the new light fixture. Compare it with the one that's attached to the outlet box in the ceiling. If the two are the same size and shape, you can hang the new fixture from the old mounting bar. However, if they're different, unscrew and discard the old mounting bar, but save the two screws; you'll need them in the next step.

8 **ATTACH THE NEW MOUNTING BAR.** Thread the two long screws provided into the holes in the new mounting bar. Be sure to put the screws in through the back of the bar. Then, use the two small screws removed from the old mounting bar to fasten the new bar to the outlet box.

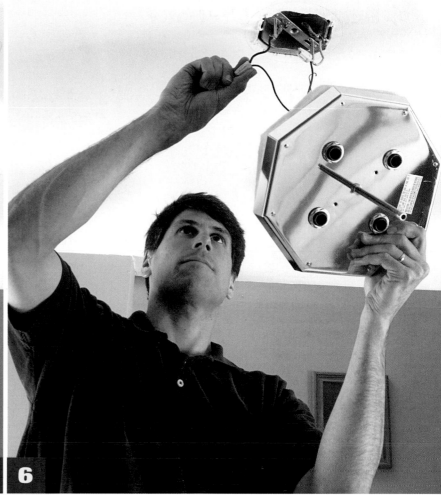

5 **6**

7 **8**

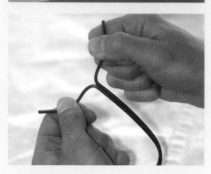

Light fixtures are often prewired with lamp cord, which is a single cable containing two bundles of twisted copper wires. It's so named because it's commonly used as the power cord on table lamps. Before stripping off the insulation, you must first peel apart the cable by hand to create the two wires. Don't use a knife to separate the cable; it's too easy to accidentally slice into one of the wires.

When tightening a wire under the head of a screw, be sure to wrap the wire once around the screw's shaft in a clockwise direction. If you wind it around in the opposite direction, the wire will be pushed out from underneath the screw head as you tighten the screw.

Hello New Chandelier!

9 **STRIP OFF THE WIRE'S INSULATION.** Cover the top of your ladder with a soft cloth and set the chandelier on top. Note that the brown lamp cord coming out of the fixture is actually two bundles of stranded copper wires. Grab the end of the cord and pull apart the two bundles to form two separate insulated wires. Then, use wire strippers to cut away ½ in. of rubber insulation from the end of each wire.

10 **MAKE THE WIRE CONNECTIONS.** Lift the chandelier close to the ceiling and join together the wires with twist-on connectors. Join one of the lamp-cord wires to the black wire coming from the outlet box and connect the other one to the white wire.

11 **ATTACH THE GROUND WIRE.** Next, take the fixture's bare copper ground wire and wrap it clockwise around the head of the green grounding screw on the mounting bar. Securely tighten the screw with a slotted screwdriver. Give a gentle tug on the ground wire and on each twist-on connector to ensure there aren't any loose connections.

12 **SECURE THE CHANDELIER.** Hold the chandelier up to the ceiling and align the holes in its canopy with the two screws protruding down from the mounting bar. Next, press the canopy tight to the ceiling and thread the tiny ball-shaped knobs onto the ends of the mounting screws. Insert three 40-watt or 60-watt Type B-10 chandelier bulbs into the sockets. Now for the moment of truth: Turn the power back on, flip the wall switch and stand back to admire your brand-new entryway light.

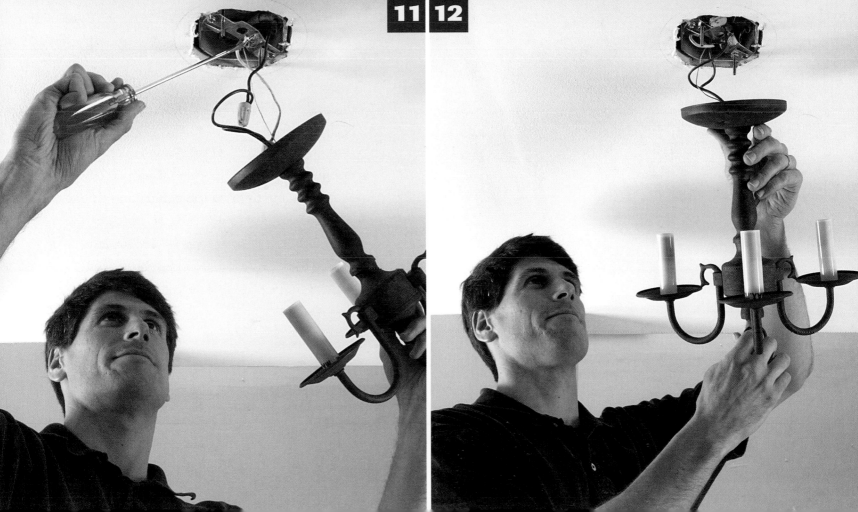

9 10
11 12

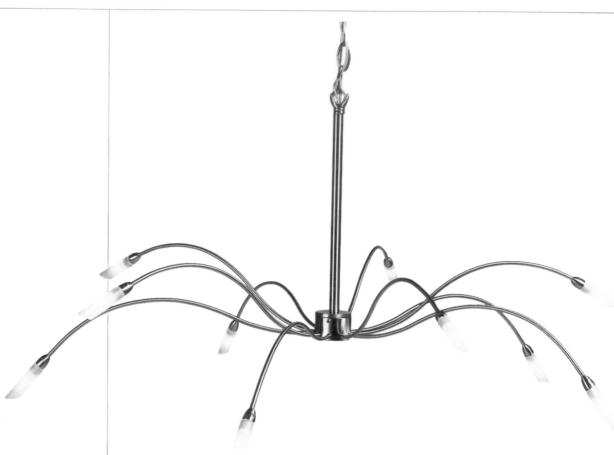

In a small foyer like this one, two smaller fixtures are better than one large one. The rectangular form of the fixtures plays off the windowpanes in the door and the geometry of the stairway.

Upgrading an entryway light is a great opportunity to make a style statement. That's probably why some lighting manufacturers offer more than 100 different entryway fixtures in their catalogs. Choosing what looks good should involve not just your own sense of style, but also the size, style, trim details, and colors that prevail in your entry area.

An entry with an 8-ft. ceiling can accommodate fixtures up to 14 in. tall; a 9-ft. ceiling can handle a fixture that's about 26 in. tall. If the entryway has a 12-ft. or 16-ft. ceiling, then consider a large hanging chandelier. There should be at least 16 in. of clearance between the fixture and the nearest wall (although 24 in. of clearance looks better). A final bit of advice: Think beyond the entry. Many of the fixtures shown here would look good elsewhere in your house.

Bright isn't always right when it comes to metal finishes on light fixtures. The flat black finish on this pair of entry lights looks great with the golden-hued oak woodwork.

Designed to hang about 20 in. from the ceiling, this pendant fixture is ideal for medium-size foyers with 9-ft. or higher ceilings. It features an inverted etched glass bowl, carved acanthus leaf details, and an antique finish.

This elaborate chandelier has the height, the detail, and the distintictive design to serve as a showpiece in a formal, two-story entryway.

Polished steel and gracefully sculpted plastic are good ingredients to look for when you want a high-tech, non-traditional impression in your entry.

A wall-mounted entry light can be just as dramatic as a ceiling-mounted fixture. Here, bright light from the fixture gets toned down as it's reflected off the wall.

A stained glass chandelier creates an Arts & Crafts ambience. But since the illumination will be subtle and slight, you may need additional light from another fixture.

Perfect for an 8-ft. ceiling, this polished-brass, flush-mounted fixture is very similar to the small chandelier shown on p. 23.

You can rely on electricity but still enjoy the look of candles with fixtures inspired by old-fashioned lanterns. Fixtures suspended by chains are great for entryways with high ceilings.

Bath Vanity Revival

Brighten the bathroom view with a **MULTILIGHT** fixture that's easy to install

THE LIGHT FIXTURE THAT'S COMMONLY INSTALLED above a bathroom vanity must do much more than simply illuminate the room. You want this fixture to make a style statement, but it also has to provide bright, even light in the vanity area. Size is important, too. The fixture should fit the space. If your bathroom has an outdated light, this upgrade will make a big difference in function and feel. Another bonus: You'll be done in about an hour.

PREP WORK REMOVING THE LIGHT WIRE CONNECTIONS INSTALLING THE FIXTURE

⊛ WHAT'S DIFFERENT?

You can install either frosted or clear incandescent bulbs in a bath vanity fixture. Frosted bulbs produce a softer, more diffused light; clear bulbs emit a bright, clean light. A clear bulb looks best in a thick, opaque shade. Try a frosted bulb in a clear shade.

◼ LINGO

Wire is the word commonly used to describe the thin metal strand that runs through plastic insulation and carries electrical current. But the proper electrical term for a wire is a *conductor*.

Tools & Gear

It doesn't take much to gear up for this project. In fact the items listed below will enable you to remove and install just about any bath vanity fixture.

TONGUE-&-GROOVE PLIERS. A pair of 8-in. or 10-in. pliers is indispensable for loosening and tightening various nuts and bolts.

RATCHET WRENCH. A ratchet wrench with appropriate-size sockets will enable you to unbolt the base of the old light from the wall. Alternatively, you can use an adjustable wrench.

SCREWDRIVERS. You'll need a small slotted screwdriver and a No. 2 Phillips. Better yet: Grab a multi-tip screwdriver designed to hold different tips.

WIRE STRIPPERS. In most cases, the fixture's wires will come pre-stripped. But just in case they're not, be sure to have a pair of wire strippers handy.

TAPE MEASURE. Used to ensure that the new fixture is parallel with the ceiling; you could also use a yardstick.

PROTECTIVE CLOTH. Cover the vanity top with a thick blanket or towel to protect it from scratches and to catch any dust.

PLASTIC SHEETING. Use painter's tape to secure plastic sheeting to the wall directly beneath the fixture. Allow the plastic to drape down over the medicine chest and onto the covered vanity top.

COOL TOOL

Electrical work requires removing and installing lots of tiny screws, which are easy to drop and lose. Magnetic-tip screwdrivers are useful for some jobs, but all too often you've got to reach deep into an electrical box or past several wires and the screw gets knocked off the tool. End the frustration with a screw-holding screwdriver. This unique tool has a pair of spring-loaded metal jaws that grab the screw head and securely hold it in place.

Shopping Tips

Whether you're shopping at your local home center, a lighting supply store, or on-line, you'll find dozens of bathroom light fixtures in a wide range of sizes, styles, and finishes. While you're paying attention to style details, here are some other considerations that will help you find the "perfect" bathroom light.

1| The fixture should be about the same length as the width of the medicine chest or mirror hanging below it. A 16-in.-long fixture mounted above a 36-in.-wide mirror will look puny and inadequate.

2| If you see a fixture that you like, but it's not quite the proper length or the desired color, ask the salesperson to show you the manufacturer's catalog. Fixtures typically come in a variety of sizes and finishes. For example, the four-light fixture we installed for this project is also available as a shorter, three-light model (shown below with a darker finish).

3| Check the depth or "extension" of the fixture, which is the distance it projects off the wall. Most baths look best with a fixture that extends no more than about 8 in.

4| It may sound crazy, but ask if the fixture can be installed upside down. Many bath fixtures can be inverted. That's a convenient option; it allows you to easily change the look of the fixture without replacing it.

5| Ask if the fixture accepts universal glass shades. If not, you might have trouble finding an affordable replacement if one breaks.

COMPONENTS & CONNECTIONS

Outlet box
(flush with wall)

Wire
connector

Fixture
mounting bar

Bare copper
ground wire

Green
grounding screw

Nipple

Arm

Thumb
screw

Socket

Cap nut

Canopy

Glass
shade

Retaining
ring

Bulb

Select your size. Many vanity lights are available in different multiples of the same size.

❖ COOL TOOL

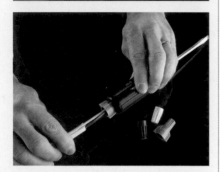

This cleverly designed screwdriver from Ideal Industries has a wrench built into the handle that's used to twist on wire connectors. Just push the connector into the recess, insert the wires, and then rotate the screwdriver. The tool's cushioned rubber grip provides a comfortable, finger-saving way to twist on the connector.

Out with the Old

1 **PREP THE SITE.** Replacing a bath vanity light fixture isn't a very messy job, but it's still a good idea to protect the mirrored medicine chest, sink, and vanity top from dust and scratches. Start by clearing the vanity top of all bath accessories. Then, cover the medicine chest with plastic sheeting. Use painter's tape to secure the sheet to the wall. Lay a thick blanket or towel across the vanity top. Now, go to the main electrical panel and turn off the power to the bathroom.

2 **REMOVE THE GLASS SHADES.** Before attempting to unbolt the fixture from the wall, remove the glass shades. For this particular light, we had to twist off a small knurled screw from the bottom of each shade. On other fixtures, you must first remove the bulbs in order to reach the retaining rings, which hold the shade in place. Once the shades are off, use pliers to loosen the cap nuts that secure the face of the fixture to the mounting plate.

3 **DISASSEMBLE THE OLD LIGHT.** Pull the face of the fixture free from the mounting plate that's bolted to the wall. Lower the fixture to expose the wires. Then, brush away any dust or debris that you find trapped inside the mounting plate.

4 **DISCONNECT THE WIRES.** Twist off the wire connectors from the ends of the wires to disconnect the fixture. Now use a ratchet wrench and socket to loosen the two nuts that hold the mounting plate to the outlet box inside the wall.

1

2

3

4

Put Up the New Light

5 **MOUNT THE BAR.** If there's some discoloration where the old fixture used to be, remove it with a damp sponge. Next, locate the new fixture's flat metal mounting bar and hollow threaded nipple.

Compare the new mounting bar with the one that's still attached to the outlet box. If they're identical, reuse the old bar. If they're different, remove the old mounting bar and install the new one. Then thread the nipple into the center hole of the mounting bar.

6 **INSTALL THE FIXTURE.** Hold up the new fixture and use twist-on wire connectors to join together the two white wires, and then the two black wires. Tighten the bare copper ground wire to the green grounding screw on the mounting bar, as illustrated on p. 39.

Press the fixture to the wall, making sure the hollow nipple passes through the center hole. Thread the round cap nut onto the nipple and tighten it by hand to hold the fixture in place.

7 **ATTACH THE GLASS SHADES.** Before installing the glass shades, unthread the retaining rings from the four sockets. Hold one of the opaque-glass shades up to the socket. Reach inside the shade and thread the retaining ring onto the socket. Don't release the shade until you're certain that the ring is properly installed. Repeat this procedure for the three remaining shades, then install four 75-watt lightbulbs.

8 **CLEAN UP AND SHOW OFF.** Turn the power back on, then flip the wall switch to light up your work. Except for a few cleanup details, you're done. To make this fixture more versatile, replace a standard toggle wall switch with a dimmer switch. Then you can turn up the brightness level for applying makeup or lower it to create a night-light.

5

6

7

8

As rooms go, the bathroom is a small space; but you can still make a big style statement. One way to do so is with new vanity lighting. Visit a nearby lighting showroom or home center and discover dozens of attractive fixtures that are specifically designed for installation over a bath vanity. Here's a small sampling of the many fixtures you'll see.

Top: These elegant (and flattering) sidelights echo the styling of the pedestal sink.

Bottom: Don't look for a vanity in this family room—this photo is here to show you that wall-mounted light fixtures can quickly add flair to any space.

Most bath vanity fixtures offer a unique design option that you won't find with any other type of light: You can completely change their appearance in a matter of minutes—without repainting or replacing them. For example, here we replaced the opaque alabaster shades of the four-light fixture shown on the previous pages with ones made of clear glass to create a fixture that's visually lighter and more subtle.

Like many bath fixtures, this one can be installed with shades facing up or down. On the previous pages, the shades are facing down; here, simply turning the fixture upside-down allows the upsweeping arms to reach gracefully upwards. In this inverted position the fixture also emits a flattering indirect light that bounces off the ceiling. Choose the look you want.

Choose fixtures that add to a bathroom's ambience. This Mexican-style bathroom filled with rich colors and textures gets even more sparkle from ice-cream-cone shaped lenses on wall-mounted fixtures.

His-and-her sinks demand equal access to light, especially with sinks divided by a medicine cabinet. Mirrored doors help reflect light sideways to banish shadows from faces.

The low ceiling in this bathroom doesn't allow for a light over the mirror, so two sidelights do the task, with a window adding a boost of light during the day.

Dark walls demand extra lighting. Here, delicately fluted glass shades and a burnished-brass finish define a three-light fixture and complementary wall sconces.

Sometimes those movie-star bulbs are just what's needed to brighten a family bathroom. These line up to share star billing with an impressive row of hats.

A single light will be just fine when space is tight, as there's less to illuminate. Here, a simple fixture allows the mirrored window sash to play a starring role.

Sometimes a new light needs an old look. The steel structure of this fixture has a forged-iron finish. Ember-glow glass shades complete the impression.

Recessed Light Retrofit

Tired of that old ceiling light? Achieve a LOW-PROFILE, HIGH-STYLE solution with a "can" light that's easy to customize

O F ALL THE LIGHTS YOU CAN INSTALL in your home, none is as versatile or as useful as a recessed light. Designed to be installed flush with the ceiling, these inconspicuous fixtures can be placed in virtually any room to provide ambient, task, or accent lighting. For this project, we'll show you how to remove an old surface-mounted hallway light and replace it with a recessed fixture that's designed for use in an insulated ceiling. If you'd like to install a different size fixture than the one shown here, go ahead. The step-by-step installation details will be the same.

PREP STEPS	PRYING WORK	OLD CEILING / NEW HOLE	MAKING CONNECTIONS

Tools & Gear

You'll only need a few basic hand tools to complete this project. In fact, you won't even need wire strippers or twist-on wire connectors; the wires on recessed fixtures come prestripped, and you can reuse the wire connectors you remove from the old light. If you don't own the tools listed below, buy or borrow them. They'll make the job much easier.

DRYWALL SAW. This compact handsaw has a short, stiff blade that's designed for making straight or curved cuts in gypsum wallboard. The saw's pointed blade can be poked through the gypsum board, allowing you to make cutouts.

FLAT PRYBAR. Long, thick prybars are ideal for demolition work, but this job calls for a more delicate tool. You'll need a small prybar with a thin, flat blade to pry the old electrical box from the ceiling.

SCREWDRIVERS. You'll need two screwdrivers—a small slotted and a No. 2 Phillips—to remove the old light and connect the new fixture.

DROP CLOTH. Spread a blanket or canvas drop cloth onto the floor to protect the flooring and to catch any dust or debris that falls from the ceiling.

PLASTIC SHEETING. To contain the drywall dust, cover adjacent doorways, windows, and heating/air-conditioning vents with inexpensive plastic sheeting.

WHAT'S DIFFERENT?

When there's no isulation in the ceiling, you can install a "non-IC" (non-insulated ceiling) recessed light, shown at right, above. But if space overhead is insulated (an attic space with insulation between ceiling joists, for example) look for an "IC" fixture, which has a protective housing.

Shopping Tips

Shopping for recessed fixtures is slightly more complicated than for other types of lighting. The can-shaped fixture housing is purchased separately from the trim kit, which is the finished ring that goes against the ceiling. The particular model you select will depend on personal taste and on the installation method. Here are some guidelines to follow when buying recessed lights:

1 First, decide which size recessed fixture you'd like. They're available with diameters of 4 in., 5 in., 6 in., and 8 in.

2 Choose either an IC (insulated ceiling) fixture or a non-IC model. If the space above the ceiling is insulated, get an IC fixture.

3 Buy a "Remodeling" (aka: "old work") fixture if you'll be installing the light from below. If you have access to the space above, you can install a "new work" fixture.

4 Once you've selected the fixture, pick a trim kit. Designed to mount in the fixture housing, a trim kit comes in a variety of styles—deep-set baffle, flush lens, decorative globe, swiveling eyeball, pin-hole spot. Trim kit color options include white, black, silver, brass and copper. However, not all trim kits fit every fixture. Check the side of the fixture's box for a listing of compatible trim kits.

5 Read the label attached to the inside of the fixture to determine which size and type of bulb you need. Caution: Exceeding the recommended maximum wattage can overheat the fixture and create a fire hazard.

COMPONENTS & CONNECTIONS

For this project, we installed a 5-in.-dia., old work recessed fixture with a black baffle trim kit. It was connected to the existing nonmetallic (Romex) cable. Note that same-color wires are joined together with wire connectors: white to white, black to black. The fixture's green grounding wire is connected to the cable's bare copper wire.

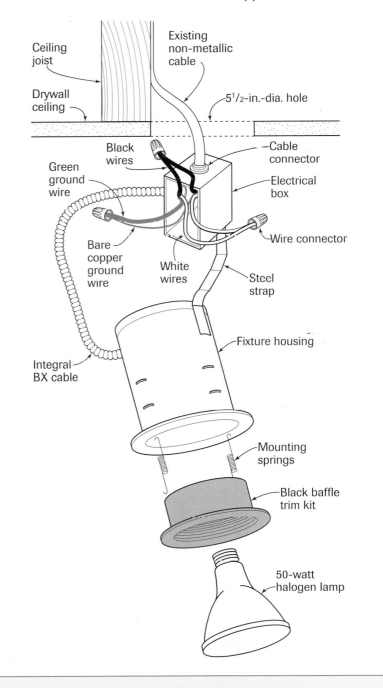

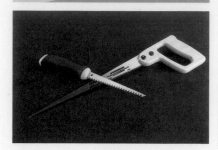

A drywall saw's short blade has large, rough-cutting teeth that create a lot of dust. A compass saw, which is often mistakenly called a keyhole saw, has a long, thin blade with smaller teeth. It doesn't cut as quickly as a drywall saw, but it will produce cleaner cuts with less dust.

Removing the Old Light

1 **PREP THE SITE.** Clear the space where you'll be working of any furniture. Next, cover the floor directly below the old light with a canvas drop cloth, moving pad, or blanket. If necessary, tape the protective cloth to the floor to prevent someone from tripping over it. Then set up a stepladder below the light fixture.

2 **CONTAIN THE DUST.** Sawing the hole in the ceiling (Step 8) is going to create a lot of fine drywall dust that you don't want to get all over the house. Cover all nearby doors, windows, and ducts with plastic sheeting. Secure the plastic with pushpins or painter's tape. Don't use regular masking tape; it has a tendency to remove paint when you peel it off. Now, go to the main electrical panel and turn off the power to the light fixture you'll be removing.

3 **UNSCREW THE OLD LIGHT.** How you remove the old light depends on what type of fixture it is. If there's a glass shade covering the fixture's base, twist off the cap located on the underside of the shade. Carefully lower the shade to reveal the two screws holding the base to the electrical box in the ceiling. Remove the screws by turning them counterclockwise. If the base of the fixture is accessible, twist off the two small knobs by hand to free the fixture from the ceiling.

4 **TWIST OFF THE WIRE CONNECTORS.** Gently pull the fixture away from the ceiling. Then, while holding the fixture with one hand, use your other hand to twist off the plastic connectors (wire nuts) from the ends of the wires.

1

2

3

4

Preparing the Ceiling

5   **REMOVE THE OLD HARDWARE.** Once you've taken down the old light, you'll likely find a flat metal strap, called the fixture-mounting bar, fastened to the electrical box. Use a screwdriver to remove the two small screws holding the bar in place. (If you're planning to save the old light fixture, keep the mounting bar, too.)

6   **PRY OUT THE ELECTRICAL BOX.** Remove the 4-in.-diameter electrical box from the ceiling. In most cases, the box will be nailed to the side of a ceiling joist. Take a flat pry bar and slip it between the box and the joist, then gently pry the box free. If the electrical box is suspended from a metal hanger bar, loosen the two screws located inside the box. Lower the box, then pry the bar from between the joists.

7   **TRACE THE TEMPLATE ONTO THE CEILING.** Take the round cardboard template that comes with the recessed fixture and use a pencil to trace its outline onto the ceiling. Hold the 5½-in.-diameter template right on the very edge of the old hole, making sure it extends away from the joist.

8   **CUT OUT THE CEILING HOLE.** Put on a pair of goggles and a dust mask. Then use a drywall saw or compass saw to cut out drywall ceiling along the pencil line. Note that you'll only be removing a crescent-shaped sliver of material. Saw carefully to avoid tearing the paper surface of the drywall.

5 **6**

7 **8**

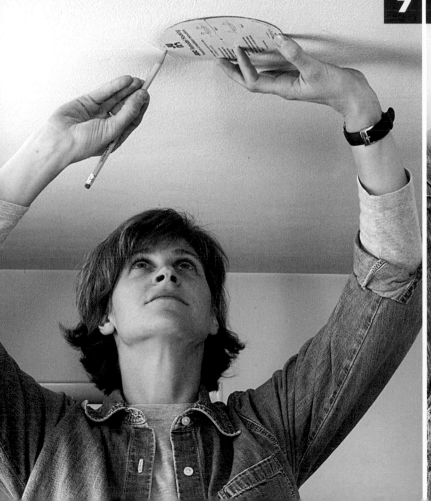

The flush trim kit, with either a white or black baffle, is by far the most popular of all the recessed-light trim kits. Both feature a low-profile white metal ring and a stepped, cone-shaped plastic baffle that fits inside. Choose the white baffle to make the fixture as inconspicuous as possible. To create more of a contrast, install the black baffle.

➕ WHAT CAN GO WRONG

If the lightbulb blinks when you flip on the switch, immediately turn it off; then shut off the electricity at the main electrical panel. The blinking light indicates that you installed either the wrong bulb or the wrong trim kit. Look inside the fixture for the label that lists appropriate trim kits and bulbs.

Installing the Fixture

9 **ATTACH THE CABLE.** Unpack the recessed light and locate the round knockout plug on the fixture's electrical box. Use a slotted screwdriver to pry out the round metal disk. Now, attach a cable connector to the knockout hole. Be sure to match the connector to the type of cable coming from the ceiling. Here, we used a nonmetallic cable connector.

10 **CONNECT THE WIRES.** Using a utility knife, cut away 6 in. of white plastic sheathing from the electrical cable; be careful not to slice into the insulated wires. Pass the cable through the knockout hole and tighten the cable connector. Then use twist-on wire connectors to join together the two black wires and the two white wires. Join the green grounding wire to the bare copper wire. Press the wires into the electrical box and snap on the metal cover.

11 **SLIP THE FIXTURE INTO THE CEILING.** Grasp the fixture with two hands and feed the cable and electrical box through the ceiling hole. Then press the round metal housing straight up into the hole until its flange is tight against the ceiling. Now reach inside the housing and push outward on the three retention clips. As each one clicks into place, it will lock the fixture fast against the drywall ceiling.

12 **INSTALL THE TRIM KIT.** Hold the baffle up to the fixture, then reach inside and hook the two mounting springs into the slots cut in the housing. The springs will pull the trim tight against the ceiling. Note that some trim kits come with leaf springs, not coil springs, as shown here. With  that type, simply push the trim straight up into the housing. Once the trim kit is installed, put in the appropriate wattage bulb, turn the power back on, and flip the light switch.

9

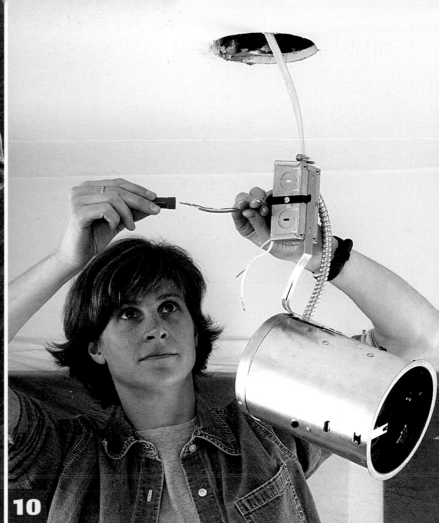

10

11

12

A single recessed fixture is often all you need in a busy or cramped space, when some extra fill or task light is called for.

Bright isn't always right. The recessed fixtures in this foyer are controlled by a dimmer switch, so the mood can be adjusted anywhere between secure and subtle.

Simple lights have a big effect. Luckily, you can install recessed lights just about anywhere—in flat or sloped ceilings, against gypsum board, plaster, or wood, and in ceilings with or without insulation. The appearance and function of each recessed light is determined by which trim kit you choose. Here's a small sampling of the many recessed light possibilities that exist around the house, including a few of the trim kits you'll find at your local home center or lighting showroom.

One light is never enough in the kitchen. The challenge when installing a run of can lights, as was done here, is to keep the installation holes in line—just a matter of careful measuring.

Recessed light fixtures are designed so that you can fit them with different "trim kits" that have specialized functions. A slotted trim kit (top left) can aim a beam of light to highlight a painting. An eyelid-type kit (top right) is often used to "wash" a wall with light while preventing excess light from being thrown back into the room. Other trim kits (bottom photos) include adjustable spotlights and floodlights.

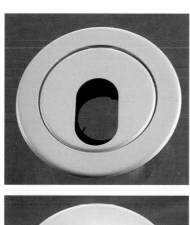

A trim kit with an angled lens can provide accent lighting, shown here. The same kit is often used in a sloped cathedral ceiling.

Controlled by a dimmer switch, these recessed lights provide task lighting as necessary. When they're turned down or turned off, they allow the hanging fixture to show off its well-crafted details.

To rescue an entryway or hallway that is cramped and dark, install a large recessed light designed to take at least a 75-watt bulb.

Don't forget the switch! Do away with dull switch-plates by shopping for some distinctive replacements. You'll find an interesting variety at your local home center.

A recessed light is often an important ingredient in any display space. This one is built into the soffit above the stairway.

Trim kits aren't about function alone. The decorative kits shown above fit 6-in. recessed fixtures. They range in height from 3 in. to 6 in., making them perfect for rooms with 8-ft. or lower ceilings.

Under-Cabinet Solution

Light up your kitchen counters with a hidden **HALOGEN LIGHT** that mounts & moves on an easy-to-install track system

LOOKING FOR A SIMPLE, YET EFFECTIVE WAY to upgrade the lighting in your kitchen? Then consider installing under-cabinet lights. These slim fixtures get fastened beneath the upper wall cabinets. From this hidden position, they bathe the countertop in light so you're never standing in shadows when chopping vegetables or reading recipes. In addition to illuminating countertop work areas, under-cabinet lights can highlight a decorative backsplash or enable you to dim down ceiling light fixtures, creating a different ambience in a very important part of the house. Here, we'll show how to install a unique low-voltage halogen light system in about 30 minutes.

COVERING THE COUNTER **INSTALLING THE LAMPS** **STAPLING THE CABLE** **PLUGGING IN**

◆ **DO IT NOW**

To see how the fixture will illuminate the counter before it's installed, lock the transformer and lamps into the track, then plug in the transformer. Hold the fixture up to the cabinet and move it around to find the location that delivers the most useful light.

✦ LINGO

All low-voltage fixtures require a transformer—an electrical device that steps down the house current, known as line voltage, from 120 volts to 12 volts.

✚ WHAT CAN GO WRONG

The average wall-mounted kitchen cabinet is built with a recessed base, which makes it easy to hide under-cabinet lights. If your wall cabinets have a flush base, you can conceal under-cabinet lights by installing a wood molding along the bottom edges of your cabinets.

Tools & Gear

The number of tools that you'll need from the list below will vary depending upon your particular kitchen. If it's not necessary to cut down the fixture's metal track to fit under the cabinet, then you won't need a hacksaw. If you don't have a staple gun, then use a hammer and needle-nose pliers to drive in small cable staples.

CORDLESS SCREWDRIVER. A cordless in-line screwdriver is lightweight and compact, making it the ideal tool for driving in the small screws that hold the track to the underside of the cabinet.

HACKSAW. If you need to cut the fixture's metal track down to size to fit your cabinets, a hacksaw will handle this cutting assignment. Make sure your saw is fitted with a sharp 18- or 24-tooth-per-in. blade.

FILE. A single-cut mill file will enable you to remove rough edges and sharp burrs that remain after sawing metal track to length.

DROP CLOTH. Protect the countertop with an old blanket or moving pad. Then, you'll have a safe place to spread out your tools and materials, without fear of scratching the counter. Get a roll of 2-in.-wide masking tape to hold the blanket in place.

CABLE STAPLES. If you don't use a staple gun (see below) to secure the power cord to the underside of the cabinet, get a box of small staples that you'll tap in with a hammer.

NEEDLE-NOSE PLIERS. Save your fingers. Use these narrow pliers to hold the staples while you hammer them in.

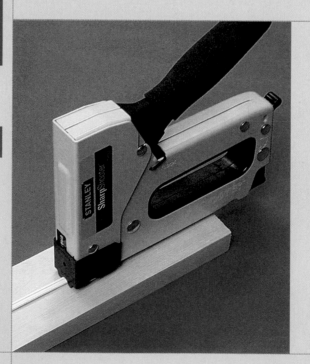

COOL TOOL

Using a standard staple gun to tack up electrical cable can put you at risk of firing a staple into electrical wires. It's better to use a cable stapler. This tool works just like a regular staple gun, but it has a special nosepiece that fits over the cable, making it impossible to pierce the wire. Many standard staple guns come with a separate cable-stapling nosepiece that you can snap on as necessary.

Shopping Tips

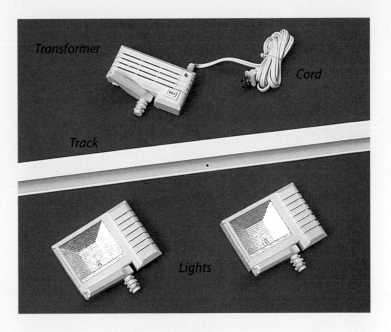

Under-cabinet lights come in different sizes and styles. In many cases, you'll be able to buy under-cabinet lights in kit form. The kit shown here contains two 20-watt quartz-halogen lights, a 30-in.-long track that the lights plug into, a 60-watt transformer, and a power cord with plug. Here are some things to consider when shopping for under-cabinet lights.

1 How bright does your light need to be? Halogen lights are usually brighter than fluorescents. If you have other lights in your kitchen, lower wattage may be fine under your cabinets.

2 Do you want dimmer-controlled lights? If so, tell your salesperson to show you lights that can be controlled by a dimmer switch.

3 Measure your under-cabinet space before you shop. Keep in mind that the under-cabinet space is not the same as the width of the cabinet.

4 Measure the recess under the cabinet. It shouldn't be less than the thickness of your light fixture.

5 Mini track lights offer the most flexibility. The fixture installed here is a track unit that allows you to quickly and easily move each track-mounted light around.

6 Some under-cabinet lights are only available as hard-wired types. They must be connected directly to an electrical cable and can't simply be plugged into an outlet. Hard-wiring your lights will take longer than doing a plug-in installation, and you might have to call in an electrician.

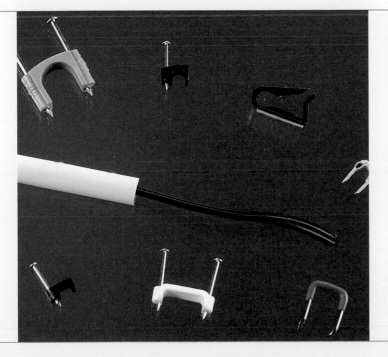

WHAT'S DIFFERENT?

Staples for installing electrical cable come in a wide variety of sizes. Make sure your staples are sized to fit the cable you plan to install. Another way to manage cable installation is to use plastic wire molding, also shown at left. This hollow molding has a self-stick backing and a cover that snaps shut after you've placed the cable inside.

Setting Up

1 **CLEAR OUT THE CABINET.** Start by emptying out all the dishes, cups, and other items that are stored on the bottom shelf of the cabinet. Pack them in a box or stack them out of the way at a safe distance from the work area. No need to empty out any of the upper shelves.

2 **PROTECT THE COUNTER.** Cover the countertop directly below the cabinet with an old blanket, canvas drop cloth, or moving pad. Fold the blanket so that it extends from the front edge of the counter all the way to the backsplash wall. Then tape it down with masking tape.

3 **MEASURE THE CABINET.** Measure the distance across the bottom of the cabinet, where the light fixture eventually will be installed. Place the end of the measuring tape against the inside of the cabinet's side panel. If you're planning to center the fixture on the cabinet, find and mark the center point of the cabinet, too.

4 **CUT THE TRACK TO FIT.** If necessary, use a hacksaw to cut the metal track down to fit the width of the cabinet. Unscrew the plastic cap from the end of the track and clamp or have a helper hold the track securely as you make the cut. Smooth away any rough burrs with a file, then replace the end cap.

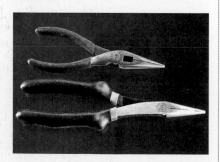

1

2

3

4

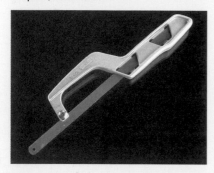
Installing the Fixture

5 **INSTALL THE TRACK.** Hold the fixture's metal track against the bottom of the cabinet. Slide it forward, toward you, until it butts up against the protruding frame that runs along the front of the cabinet. Then secure the track to the cabinet with the two short screws provided.

6 **ATTACH THE LAMPS.** Take one of the halogen lamps and rotate its locking arm to the open position, which is perpendicular to the glass lens. Hold the lamp up to the track and firmly push it into the track's channel. Rotate the locking arm down to the closed position to securely lock the lamp to the track. Attach other lamps in the same manner.

7 **INSTALL THE TRANSFORMER.** Attach the transformer to the track using the same procedure as described in Step 6: Swing the transformer's locking arm to the open position, slip it into the track, then close the arm to lock the transformer in place. Keep in mind that the transformer and lamps can be positioned anywhere on the track.

8 **STAPLE UP THE WIRE.** Using ½-in.-long staples, attach the transformer's power cord to the back panel or underside of the cabinet. Don't drive the staples into the wall below the cabinet; they'll easily pull loose from the gypsum wallboard or plaster.

5

6

7

8

+ WHAT CAN GO WRONG

If the lamps don't come on when you press the switch, and you know the bulbs are good, then you may have tripped the ground-fault circuit interrupter (GFCI) on the outlet or at the circuit breaker. Press the "reset" button to resume the flow of electricity.

◆ DO IT NOW

Most under-cabinet lights come with bulbs, but read the packaging to find out for sure. And when you buy your lights, get at least two extra bulbs.

Let There Be Light!

9 **CONTROL THE EXCESS WIRE.** At 6 ft. long, the transformer's power cord is long enough to reach an outlet. In fact, in most cases, you'll have plenty of extra wire. Rather than winding up the excess wire into an unwieldy knot, stretch it out along the underside of the cabinet and then double it back toward the nearest outlet. Secure the wire with staples spaced 8 in. to 10 in. apart.

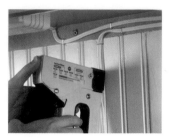

10 **PLUG IN THE TRANSFORMER.** For the neatest appearance, run the wire straight down to the outlet, placing the nearest staple about 6 in. from the plug. Push the plug into the outlet and then flip on the switch that's located on the transformer. Note that the rocker switch has three positions: high, low, and off.

11 **REPLACE A FAULTY BULB.** If you need to replace one of the quartz halogen bulbs, start by carefully sliding out the glass lens. Then, use a soft cloth to grab the bulb and firmly pull it out of the lamp. If you use your bare fingers, natural skin oil can get on the bulb and possibly cause it to crack when it gets hot. Push the replacement bulb into the lamp, again using the cloth to grab it.

12 **MAKING FINAL ADJUSTMENTS.** Flip on the switch and then stand back to view the lighting pattern created by the two lamps. If the counter isn't evenly illuminated or if you'd prefer more light in one specific spot, unplug the fixture and reposition the lamps on the track.

9 **10**

11 **12**

The low-voltage quartz fixtures shown below are easy to install on the underside of a wall cabinet. They're also popular for use inside bookcases, display cases, and cabinets that have glass doors.

This compact fluorescent light has its own switch. You can also buy models designed to be hardwired to an existing circuit and models that plug into wall outlets.

Function is the key when you're choosing under-cabinet lights. It's more about how they work and what they do than about style. Don't worry—you've still got some choices.

Compact fluorescent lights are the most common—and affordable—type of under-cabinet fixture sold today. They come as thin as 1 in. wide and in a variety of lengths, ranging from 12 in. to 48 in. long.

Miniature disk lights come in different sizes and can be used under or inside a cabinet. These "hockey puck lights" can either be surface-mounted or flush-mounted.

Open-face strip lights contain rows of evenly spaced xenon bulbs mounted on a ¾-in.-square aluminum channel.

Flexible rope lights offer an easy and affordable way to add accent lighting to the space below, above, or inside a cabinet.

An under-cabinet fluorescent fixture casts a broad band of softly diffused light. Note how it illuminates both the countertop and the backsplash wall.

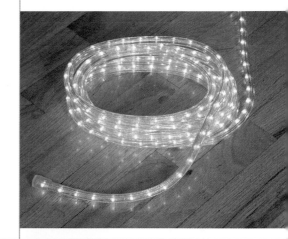

Rope lighting is compact enough to be used under your cabinets, but it's fun to use elsewhere, too. The rope is actually a length of clear vinyl tubing filled with tiny bulbs. The bulbs are surprisingly bright, and the tubing is flexible enough to snake around corners and over obstructions. You can buy it by the foot or in precut lengths, either ready to plug in or to hard-wire to an existing circuit.

Installed under every cabinet, the low-profile lights in this remodeled kitchen can work on their own or with overhead track lights to provide ample task lighting.

Sometimes it just takes a single under-cabinet light fixture to make a big difference. Though it can require extra work, hard-wiring your under-cabinet lights gives the completed installation a cleaner look, as shown here.

In this kitchen, a hand-painted tile backsplash called for under-cabinet lights that could draw attention to this unique detail. Positioning the under-cabinet lights close to the wall provides a wash of light to illuminate the scene.

Fluorescent fixtures like this one deliver a generous amount of light but demand very little power.

Some under-cabinet lights are so small they can go just about anywhere. This low-profile light is barely visible, centered under the top shelf.

Right on Track

With a new **TRACK LIGHTING** system, you'll have light
that's easy to control and customize

TRACK LIGHTING, FIRST POPULAR more than three decades ago, is
making a strong comeback thanks to a new generation of sleek
fixtures that come in a wide array of shapes, colors, and styles.
And while basic straight track systems are still available, you'll
also find curved track and track that can divide and turn corners. No matter where you install track lighting, it's nice to know that you'll
always be able to change fixtures, aim light in different directions, and tune
your lighting scheme whenever the urge strikes. The tools and step-by-step
techniques featured in this project will work for any track lighting system
you choose. Let's get started!

| REMOVING THE OLD LIGHT | CONNECTING THE WIRES | HANGING THE TRACK | THE FINISHED LOOK |

Tools & Gear

There are surprisingly few tools required to install track lighting, but the job will be much easier if you have on hand the items listed below. A cordless drill/driver is particularly effective for quickly removing the old fixture and attaching the new track to the ceiling. The drywall saw is needed only if you must cut in a shallow pancake-style ceiling box.

LINESMAN PLIERS. These heavy-duty pliers are indispensable for cutting cable, twisting together wires, and tightening nuts.

MULTITIP SCREWDRIVER. For removing and tightening the various screws—Phillips and slotted—that you'll encounter when removing the old light and connecting the new one.

PUTTY KNIFE. A flexible-blade, 1½-in.-wide putty knife is needed to patch holes in the ceiling with spackling compound.

CORDLESS DRILL/DRIVER. This battery-powered tool is used to drill holes and to drive in and back out screws.

DRYWALL SAW. If it's necessary to install a pancake box to support the new fixture, use this small handsaw to cut the 4-in.-dia. hole in the drywall ceiling.

WIRE STRIPPERS. Use this electrician's tool to cut and strip wire.

TAPE MEASURE. Needed to determine the exact positioning of the track on the ceiling.

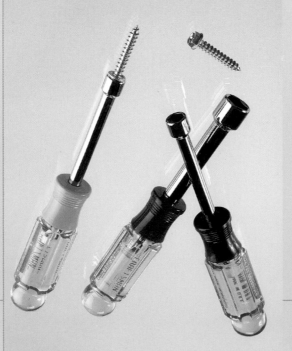

COOL TOOL

Nut drivers aren't nearly as popular as screwdrivers, but they should be. These highly underrated tools are invaluable for quickly removing and tightening hex-head nuts and bolts. They're particularly effective in tight spots where you can't fit a wrench. Nut drivers are sold individually and in multipiece sets that include sizes ranging from ³⁄₁₆ in. to ½ in. Color-coded handles make it easy to identify the different sizes.

Shopping Tips

Ordering a track lighting system is fun because you get to mix and match the parts to create a custom lighting scheme that suits the location and your sense of style. Another benefit is that all of the parts get packaged in a ready-to-install kit. The key is to make sure that you order all the necessary pieces and that all the components are compatible. Here's a list of the parts we used for this project (see photo at right):

1 | TRANSFORMER WITH COVER. This large, round device gets mounted to the ceiling directly over the electrical box. A 300-watt transformer can handle up to six 50-watt light fixtures.

2 | TRACK ASSEMBLY. The two curved aluminum rails connect to the transformer to create an 8-ft.-long S-shaped track.

3 | STANDOFF SUPPORTS. A pair of 4-in.-long supports is used to suspend the outer ends of the aluminum rails from the ceiling.

4 | LIGHT FIXTURES. Shown here are six 50-watt fixtures with cobalt blue glass shades. They represent just one of the many designs and colors available.

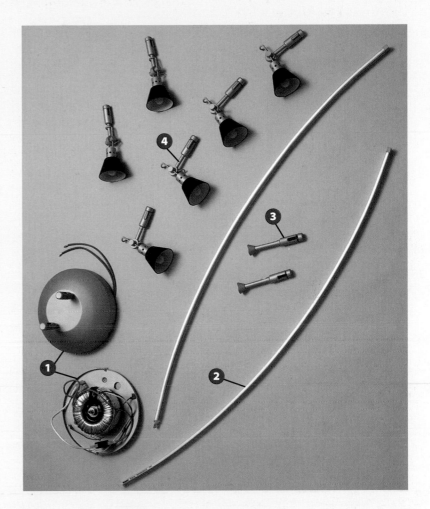

THREE OF A KIND

Looking for the most affordable, easiest-to-install track light? Then go to a lighting showroom or home center and ask for a stock three-light kit. In one box you'll get everything you need to install the fixture, even the mounting screws. The traditional-style kit shown at left includes two 2-ft.-long tracks, a straight connector, and three 50-watt round-back fixtures, which have black baffles.

Getting Started

1 REMOVE THE BULBS. First, go to the main electrical panel and turn off the power to the light fixture that you're replacing. Confirm that it's off by flipping the wall switch. Then, stand on a safe, sound ladder and remove the glass shade or plastic diffuser and lightbulbs from the existing fixture. Carefully hand the parts down to a helper.

2 DISCONNECT THE WIRES. Next, lower the fixture's canopy to expose the wire connections. If you're removing a fluorescent light, as shown here, reveal the wires by snapping off the long metal cover attached to the center of the fixture. Twist off the plastic wire connectors from the ends of the wires.

3 UNSCREW THE OLD LIGHT. Find and remove the screws holding the base of the fixture to the ceiling. Keep a firm grip on the fixture as you're backing out the screws. Then carefully lower the fixture down to a helper. Remove all the old parts from the room to eliminate any possible tripping hazards.

4 PATCH THE CEILING. Before proceeding any further, inspect the ceiling for any screw holes, peeling paint, or damage. Fill all holes, scratches, and gouges with spackling compound. Once the compound has dried, sand the surface smooth and apply a coat of primer and topcoat paint.

⊛ WHAT'S DIFFERENT?

Most low-voltage track lighting fixtures accept two types of bi-pin halogen bulbs. The MR16 bulb (top, left) emits a bright, pure-white beam of light. The tiny T4 bulb (top, right) fits inside of a small frosted-glass shade. It produces a softer, more diffused light. Each bulb is rated for 2,000 hours and available in 20-watt, 35-watt, and 50-watt sizes.

⠿ LINGO

In the vernacular of track lighting, the term *pendant* refers to a fixture that hangs down from the track by a cable or rigid metal stem. Pendant fixtures come in several colors and styles, but they can't be aimed so they're best for direct downlight situations.

Install the Transformer

5 **ADD A CEILING BOX.** Chances are there will be an electrical outlet box mounted in the ceiling. If there is none, you must install one to support the new fixture. Use a drywall saw to cut a 4-in.-dia. hole in the ceiling directly over a joist. Then, using a cordless drill, fasten

a shallow pancake box to the joist with the two screws provided. Pull the existing electrical cable through the cable connector and knockout hole in the box. Attach a flat mounting bar to the box.

6 **INSTALL THE CANOPY.** Next, take the bare copper ground wire coming from the ceiling and tighten it under the green grounding wire on the mounting bar. Thread the nipple (included) into the hole in the bar and secure it with a nut. Hold the round metal canopy close to the ceiling and feed the two transformer extension wires through the nipple. Use twist-on connectors to join the white and black wires coming from the ceiling to the respective white and black extension wires.

7 **SECURE THE TRANSFORMER.** Press the canopy flat against the ceiling so that the threaded nipple passes through the transformer's center hole. Secure the canopy and transformer with a washer and nut. Tighten the nut with linesman pliers.

8 **CONNECT THE WIRES.** Raise the round bowl-shaped cover up to the canopy. The wires dangling from the transformer have convenient push-on connectors. Join each of these wires to the appropriate terminal on the inside of the cover. Then, slide the cover over the canopy and secure it with the three small retaining screws provided.

❖ COOL TOOL

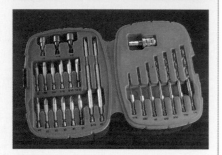

It's always more economical to purchase hand tools and power-tool accessories in multipiece kits—and this is especially true of drill bits. Look for a kit that has a durable storage case and a wide range of drill bits and screwdriving tips. This 25-piece kit has seven hex-shank drill bits, 14 screwdriving tips, three sockets, and a hex-shank adapter.

Position the Track

9 **LOCATE THE STANDOFF SUPPORTS.** Protruding from the transformer cover are two short posts, called rail adapters, which have slots that accept the curved aluminum rail sections. Have a helper hold one end of a curved rail in the rail adapter on the transformer. Slide a standoff support 4 in. to 6 in. onto the opposite end of the rail. Press the support against the ceiling and mark its location with a pencil.

10 **BORE MOUNTING HOLES.** Use a cordless drill to bore a ⅜-in.-dia. hole through the ceiling on your pencil mark. As you bore the hole, have your helper hold a vacuum-cleaner wand beside the drill bit to capture the drywall dust. Disassemble the standoff support and insert the provided toggle bolt through the support's top fitting. Pinch closed the toggle's spring-loaded wings, then use a screwdriver to push the toggle bolt through the ceiling hole.

11 **TIGHTEN THE THREADED FITTINGS.** Pull down on the aluminum fitting with one hand to create pressure on the toggle bolt inside the ceiling. Then, use a cordless drill to slowly tighten the screw until the toggle is snug against the ceiling.

12 **INSTALL THE STANDOFFS.** Take the 4-in.-long stem portion of the standoff support and thread it into the fitting that you just mounted to the ceiling. Be careful that you don't cross the threads. Now unscrew the small round cap from the bottom end of the stem to allow access to the rail slot.

9 **10**

11 **12**

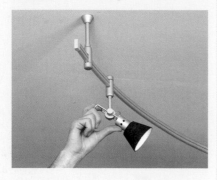
Hang the Track

13 **ATTACH THE RAIL.** With the assistance of a helper, insert one end of a curved rail into the rail adapter protruding from the transformer cover. Raise the other end of the rail into the slot in the standoff support screwed to the ceiling. Thread the small round cap onto the support to hold up the outer end of the rail.

14 **JOIN THE RAILS.** Install the second curved rail, using the same procedure as described in Step 13. Be sure that it curves in the opposite direction of the first rail to create the S-shaped track. Grab each rail where they meet at the transformer and force the ends together to create a single 8-ft.-long rail. To prevent the rail sections from separating, use a hex-key wrench to tighten the setscrews on the transformer's rail adapters.

15 **ASSEMBLE THE LIGHTS.** Each light fixture must be assembled before it can be installed on the track. Start by spreading a thick blanket or quilted moving pad across your work surface. Slide the glass shade onto the fixture's socket. Next, thread the retaining ring onto the socket to hold the shade in place. Then install a 50-watt or smaller bulb.

16 **INSTALL THE FIXTURES.** At the end of each light fixture is a small round cap and rail slot. Twist off the cap and slide the fixture any-where you'd like onto the track. Replace the cap to hold the fixture in place. Install the remaining fixtures in the same manner. If you need to move a fixture, simply loosen its cap, slide the fixture to a new spot, and retighten the cap. Finally, the moment of truth: Turn on the power, flip the switch, and begin enjoying the beauty and versatility of your new track lighting system.

13 **14**

15 **16**

This bright-white 250-watt fixture has a set of hinged barn doors, which can be opened or closed to control the light spread.

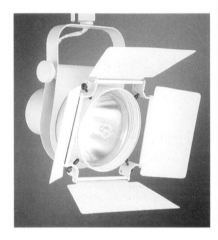

Look on the bright side of the track light: It's versatile. While every track lighting system consists of the same basic parts—a metal track and individual light fixtures—the many variations of each part create an almost limitless number of styles, color combinations, and design options. Before purchasing a track-lighting system, be sure to review the manufacturer's catalog to see which—and how many—parts are compatible with the system you're interested in. If the options are limited, check a different catalog.

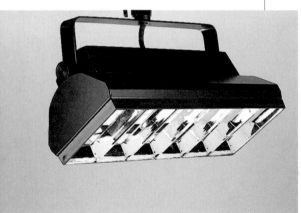

This 12-in.-long wall-wash fixture uses an energy-saving compact fluorescent bulb to shine a wide beam of soft light.

Rough-hewn beams are the focus of this kitchen ceiling, so track lights were chosen for their understated look. Most track systems also offer matching fixtures that can be mounted singly, as seen near the window at right.

A scaled-down version of industrial lighting is a good fixture choice for a small, contemporary kitchen. Low-voltage halogen lamps add sparkling warm-white ambience at night.

FUN AND FUNKY

If you want a variety of style choices with just one track-lighting system, look for one like this. The S-shaped track (shown below) will accept light units in different sizes, colors, and styles, as shown above.

Pendant kits are available for installing track lights on very high or sloping ceilings. The rigid metal stem suspends the track 6 in. to 18 in. down from the ceiling.

Designed to blend in with traditional-style rooms, this 6-in.-dia. fixture has an antique brass finish and clear prismatic glass shade.

Featuring a jet-black finish and pin-spot halogen bulb, this cone-shaped fixture is designed for a contemporary-styled home.

Called a Trapeze Pendant, this unique, cable-suspended fixture is infinitely adjustable from 10 in. to 103 in. Simply depress the buttons on the upper bar and slide the fixture up or down. It's shown with a red-glass shade, one of nine colors that are available.

TRACK-LIGHT LAYOUT PLANS

By using specially designed connectors, sections of track can be joined together to create many interesting patterns. The pattern you choose will depend on the size of the room and how many fixtures you need to properly illuminate the space. Here are three common track-lighting layouts.

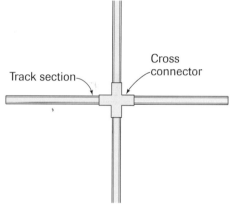

Track section

Cross connector

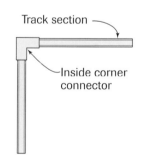

Track section

Inside corner connector

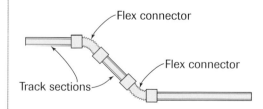

Flex connector

Flex connector

Track sections

Above: Track lighting takes on a whole new look with pendant Noguchi-style shades. These fixtures can be adjusted not only along the recessed track but also by lengthening the cords.

Left: In an artist's studio, adjustable can lights on a track system supplement the diffuse light from the glass-block window.

Chandelier Showcase

Combine a new chandelier with a decorative **CEILING MEDALLION**
to make a dramatic dining-room transformation

EVERY DINING ROOM DESERVES a distinctive chandelier. This light-giving centerpiece expresses the style and flavor that you want around your dining-room table. Whether it's formal, rustic, off-beat, intriguing, or romantic, you can bet there's a chandelier that evokes these and other qualities. It's no wonder that so many homeowners take chandeliers with them when they move, leaving inadequate substitutes behind. If you need to replace an outdated chandelier with one that suits your sense of style, this project is for you. The decorative medallion included here is a special addition that's worth considering in any chandelier project.

ASSEMBLING THE PARTS   **THE MEDALLION**   **HANGING THE FIXTURE**   **THE FINISHED LOOK**

⁙ DO IT FAST

It's best to move the dining-room table out of the way before installing the new chandelier. But if that's not possible because it's simply too heavy, cover it with a moving pad or thick blanket.

⊘ UPGRADE

A new chandelier can be just the beginning of your dining-room transformation. Chances are the manufacturer also has other light fixtures made in the same style as the chandelier. Ask to see other fixtures in the same style that you might be able to use on the wall or in the hallway or living room.

◆ DO IT NOW

Here's an easy way to keep track of all the small parts and pieces of hardware that come with a new light fixture: Take a cupcake baking tray and separate the parts into the individual cups.

Tools & Gear

Most chandeliers come partially assembled, which significantly reduces the installation time. However, there are several key parts, wires, and fittings that must be attached to complete the assembly. You'll need these tools to get the job done.

STEPLADDERS. Two are definitely better than one for this project. If you can't borrow an extra ladder from a neighbor, get a step stool that enables you to reach the ceiling.

CAULKING GUN. A caulking gun is used to apply adhesive to the back of the decorative ceiling medallion. If the medallion is made of expanded urethane foam, as ours was, be sure to buy a compatible urethane adhesive caulk.

TONGUE-&-GROOVE PLIERS. You'll need these adjustable-jaw pliers to tighten various nuts and bolts.

LINESMAN PLIERS. That's right: Make room for a second pair of pliers in your tool belt. Linesman pliers are for cutting cable and twisting wires together.

SCREWDRIVERS. You'll need two screwdrivers—a small slotted and a No. 2 Phillips—to remove the old light and connect the new fixture.

WIRE STRIPPERS. Use this handy tool to cut and strip wire.

TAPE MEASURE. Most chandeliers come with a 10-ft. to 16-ft.-long chain, which can be shortened to accommodate different ceiling heights. You'll need a tape measure to determine how long to make the chandelier's chain.

COOL TOOL

Insulated screwdrivers provide an extra measure of safety when working on electrical projects. The driver's metal shaft is sheathed in thick rubber so there's little chance of conducting electricity should you come in contact with a live wire, exposed screw terminal, or metal outlet box.

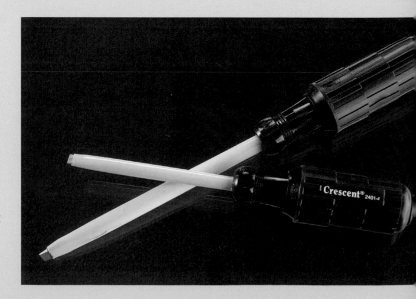

Shopping Tips

Some chandeliers are simple in design, like the one shown on p. 93, for example. But other chandeliers have many parts. (The model shown in the installation sequence and illustrated at right is a good example of a more complex chandelier.) No matter what size and style of chandelier you buy, this new fixture will come with everything you need to install it. You'll need to buy some construction adhesive if you're going to install a medallion. And when you're done, you'll need to buy bulbs designed to fit your chandelier.

Here are some shopping tips that will help you sort through the huge variety of chandeliers that are available, and find one that suits your budget and your sense of style.

1| Most lighting showrooms only have one example of each chandelier on display. However, many fixtures come in two or three different finishes or colors. Check the catalog to see if any other finishes are available.

2| If the fixture's lightbulbs are protected by shades, those shades are included with the chandelier. But some manufacturers offer a line of optional shades—in fabric and glass—that fit their chandeliers.

3| If you see a six-light chandelier that you like, but it's too small for your dining room, ask your salesperson if it's available in a larger size. Many chandeliers are made in the same style, but in different sizes. You can expect larger versions to have more lights.

4| Various chains are available for suspending the chandelier from the ceiling. You can often order them in various sizes, colors, and designs.

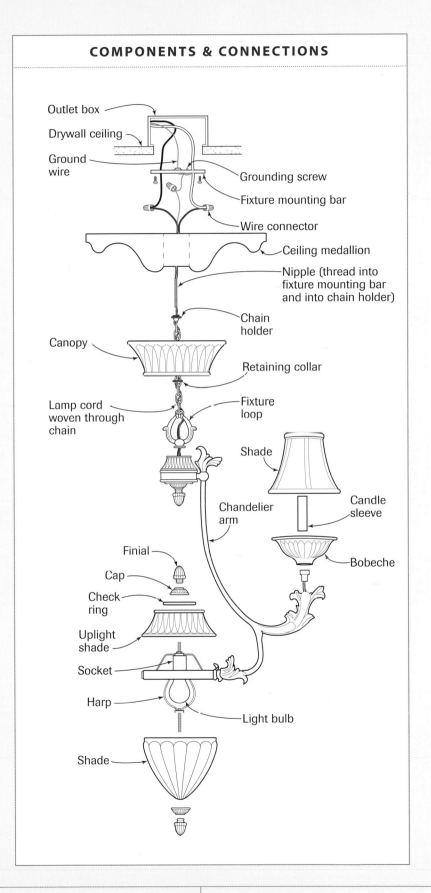

COMPONENTS & CONNECTIONS

Outlet box

Drywall ceiling

Ground wire

Grounding screw

Fixture mounting bar

Wire connector

Ceiling medallion

Nipple (thread into fixture mounting bar and into chain holder)

Chain holder

Canopy

Retaining collar

Lamp cord woven through chain

Fixture loop

Shade

Candle sleeve

Chandelier arm

Finial

Cap

Check ring

Uplight shade

Bobeche

Socket

Harp

Light bulb

Shade

Putting Parts Together

1 **ATTACH THE LOOP.** To begin, take the chandelier's lamp cord and bare copper ground wire and pass them through the hole in the base of the fixture loop. Next, thread the fixture loop onto the top of the chandelier's base, being careful not to cross the threads. Securely hand-tighten the loop. Don't use pliers.

2 **SLIP ON THE SLEEVES.** Check each of the six tall metal socket arms to be sure that they're perfectly straight. If any are bent out of alignment, carefully bend them back to an upright position. Then, slip on the six hollow plastic candle sleeves.

3 **HOOK ON THE CHAIN.** Use two pairs of pliers to bend open the end link on the chandelier's hanging chain. Slip the open link through the hole in the top of the fixture loop that's attached to the top of the chandelier. Then use the pliers to bend the link closed.

4 **THREAD THE WIRES.** Take the ends of the lamp cord and ground wire and weave them through the chain. Pass both wires through every third or fourth link—not every single link. Also, if you plan to spray-paint the ceiling medallion a decorative color, do it now so that it has time to dry before you install it.

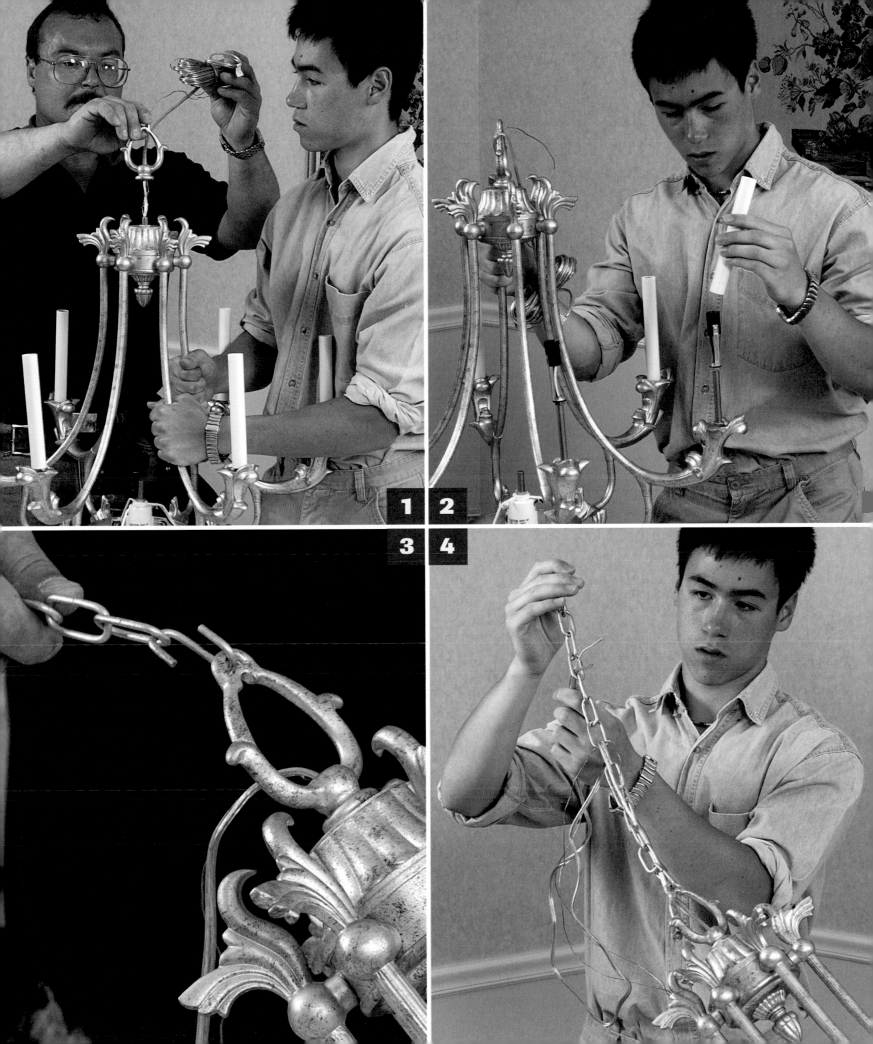

1

2

3

4

DO IT RIGHT

The chandelier comes with a 3-in.-long nipple, which is adequate when installing the fixture directly to the ceiling. But if you plan to add a ceiling medallion, the 3-in. nipple will be too short. Replace it with a 5½-in.- or 6-in.-long nipple.

ASK THE PRO

If you're not positive that the existing electrical box in the ceiling can support the weight of the new chandelier, call in an electrician for an evaluation.

Getting Set

5 **ADD THE CANOPY.** Take the end of the chain and wires and feed them through the hole in the canopy. Make sure that the wide, open end of the canopy faces away from the chandelier. Now go to the main electrical panel and turn off the electricity to the dining room.

6 **REMOVE THE OLD LIGHT.** Next, with a helper's assistance, take down the old dining-room light fixture. Unscrew and lower the canopy to access the electrical box in the ceiling. Twist off the wire connectors and remove the old fixture.

7 **PREPARE THE MEDALLION.** Apply a continuous bead of adhesive caulk to the back side of the ceiling medallion. Run the bead once around the circular medallion, making sure to keep it at least 2 in. away from the outer edge. Then, feed the lamp cord and ground wire through a 5½-in.-long hollow nipple.

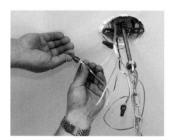

8 **WIRE THE CHANDELIER.** Screw the fixture-mounting bar to the outlet box in the ceiling. Pass the wires and nipple through the canopy and medallion. Have a helper hold up the chandelier as you make the wire connections. Tighten the ground wire coming from the outlet box to the grounding screw on the mounting bar, then connect it to the fixture's ground wire. Peel the lamp cord down the middle and strip ½ in. of insulation from the end of each wire. Use wire nuts to connect these wires to the black and white wires coming from the box.

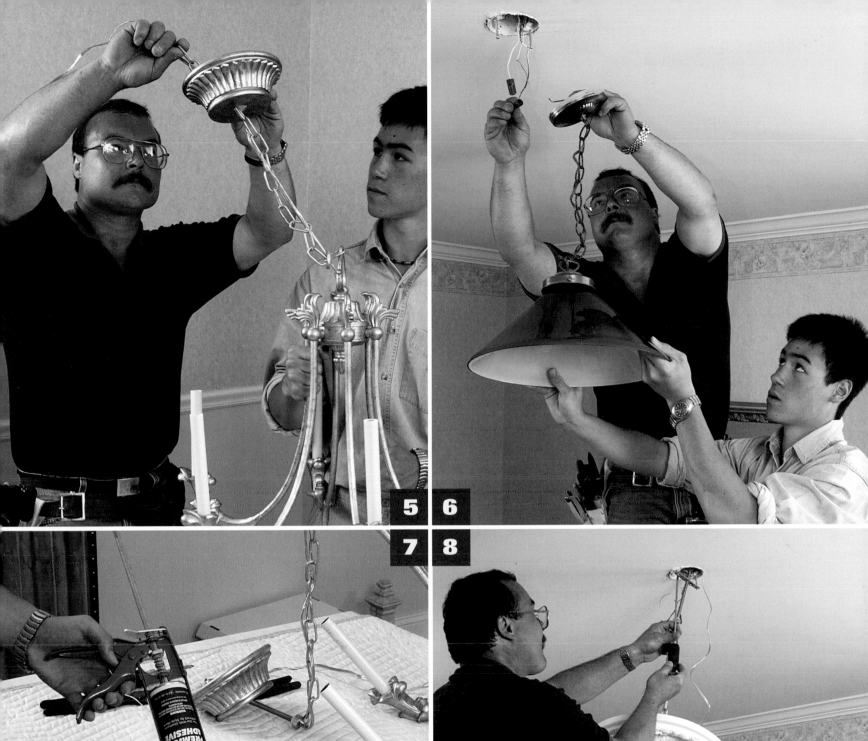

5

6

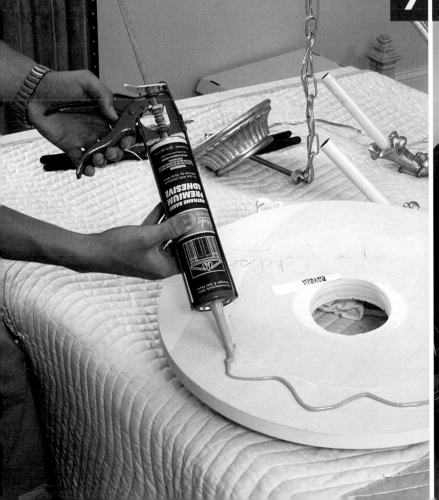

7

8

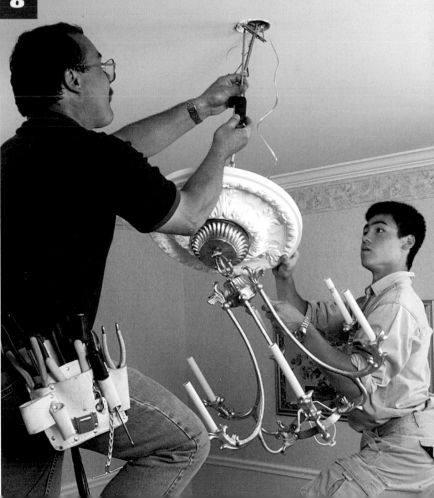

▶ DO IT RIGHT

If the chandelier is controlled by a toggle switch, replace it with a dimmer switch. You'll then be able to control the light level and set the mood for dining, conversation, or homework.

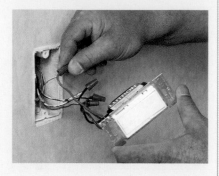

❖ COOL TOOL

For faster wire-nut connections, you can use this Spin-Twist Wire-Connector accessory in your cordless drill. Instead of twisting connectors by hand, the drill does the work for you.

Hang the Chandelier

9 **INSTALL THE MEDALLION.** Hold the medallion close to the ceiling. Center it on the outlet box, then firmly press the medallion tight against the ceiling. You'll feel the adhesive "grab" the ceiling surface. As you hold the medallion in place, have a helper slide the canopy up the chain.

10 **SECURE THE CANOPY.** Push the canopy tight against the medallion. Slide the retaining collar up the chain and thread it onto the underside of the chain holder. Use pliers to tighten the collar. The canopy and adhesive should hold the medallion in place, but if necessary, you can drive finishing nails through the medallion and into ceiling joists.

11 **ASSEMBLE THE CANDLES.** At the base of each of the chandelier's six arms is a small decorative glass dish, called a bobeche. Lower each bobeche over a candle sleeve and carefully set it down onto the arm. Then put a 40-watt or 60-watt candelabra-base lightbulb into each socket.

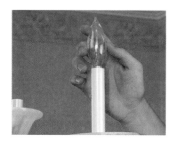

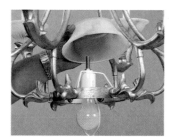

12 **COMPLETE THE ASSEMBLY.** This chandelier has an attractive accent light that resembles an urn. It consists of two glass shades and a lightbulb socket. Put a 40-watt or 60-watt lightbulb into the socket. Next, set the uplight shade on top of the socket. Install the check ring and decorative cap, then thread on the finial. Hold the downlight shade against the underside of the socket and secure it to the harp with a cap and finial. To complete this project, install the six fabric shades and then turn the power back on.

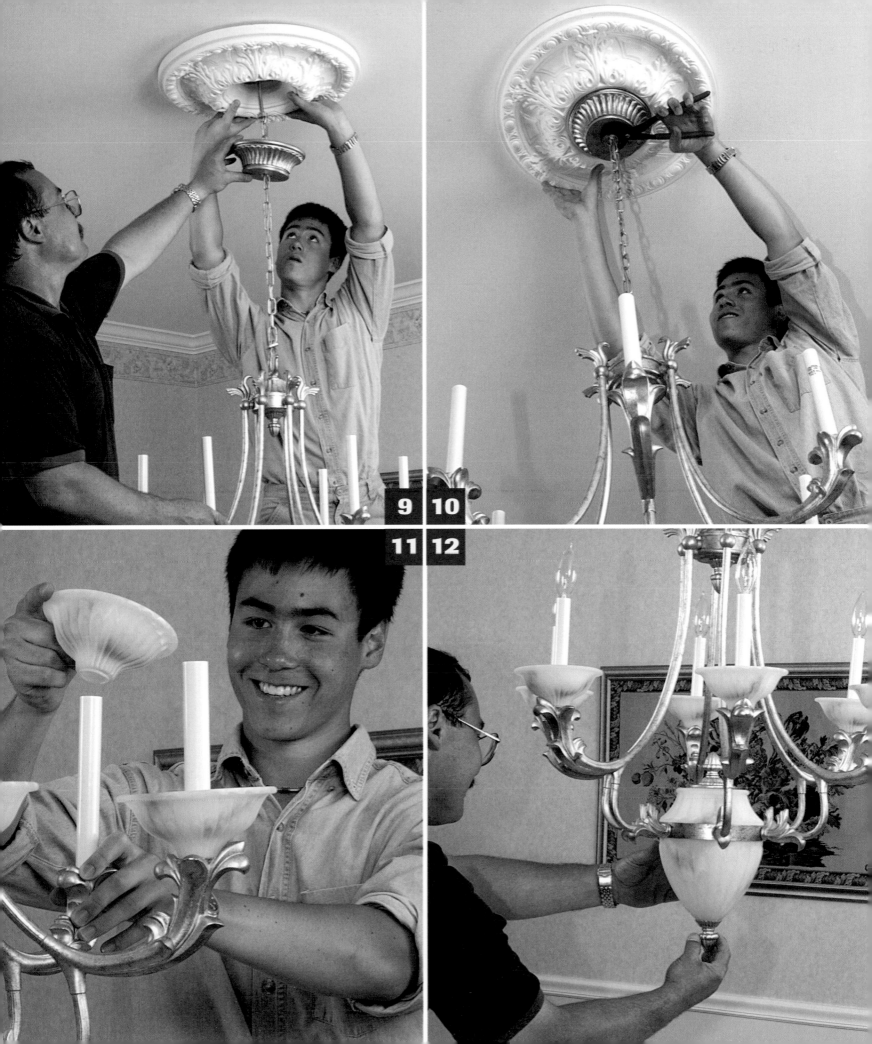

9 10
11 12

In a traditionally styled dining room, a reproduction Colonial-style chandelier provides the ambience of a bygone era without the hazards of dripping candle wax and open flames.

At just 18 in. in diameter and 20 in. high, this stunning five-light chandelier is perfect for smaller spaces. It features an attractive bronze finish and teardrop amber crystals.

There is no such thing as a typical chandelier, and that's exactly why shopping for one is so much fun. Chandeliers come in literally hundreds of different styles, sizes, shapes, and finishes. Visit a lighting showroom and you'll see a wide variety of models ranging from rustic wrought iron and antique silver to highly polished brass and gorgeous gold leaf. Many are artfully embellished with intertwining vines, twisted ropes, overlapping leaves, or sparkling crystals. It's also fun to shop at antique or second-hand stores for something special. Note, too, that some chandeliers have glass or fabric shades, while others sport bare bulbs.

A chandelier can make a dining table useful for just about any task. Dimmable fixtures like these with incandescent bulbs allow for intimate dinners and well-lit homework sessions. The chandelier is positioned high enough to stay out of the way but low enough to cast a cozy light.

This elegant chandelier keeps its six bulbs modestly shielded behind one large, translucent shade. A pendant stem—rather than a chain—complements the simplicity of the shade.

The ornate look of wrought iron complete with tendrils makes an impressive chandelier that's right in scale and style for a timber-frame house.

WINNING MEDALLIONS

Today you'd struggle to find a plaster expert who could recreate the ornate moldings that embellished many houses built during the 1920s and 1930s. But these classic molding details have inspired a vast and varied family of lightweight foam moldings that look remarkably like traditional plaster details and are surprisingly easy to install. Including a decorative medallion with your new chandelier is a great way to make this improvement even more dramatic.

If you don't use a medallion with your chandelier, it'll be finished off at the ceiling by a canopy, like this flat, black, contemporary version. Lighting catalogs don't always show canopies in photos, so ask what styles and finishes are available for your chandelier.

Make a bold statement with this handsome six-light chandelier, which measures 31 in. high by 36 in. in diameter. Its highly detailed ironwork is accented by cultured-marble glass and an aged-Etruscan finish.

This elegant, traditional-style chandelier has a rich silver finish and five jet-black fabric shades.

The Mediterranean-inspired design of this six-light chandelier is evident in its faux-rope details, Spanish alabaster-glass shades, and antique gold-leaf finish.

Picture-Perfect Pathway Lighting

Enhance the nighttime curb appeal of your home
with low-voltage **LANDSCAPE LIGHTING**

LANDSCAPE LIGHTING is the general term used to describe a large and varied family of outdoor lighting fixtures. These versatile, weatherproof lights can be used to illuminate pathways, flowerbeds, trees, fences, driveways, and other natural and man-made features. Here, we'll show how to install a series of low-voltage lights beside a brick walkway. At night, the 18-watt fixtures provide safe passage and a charming ambience. During the day, they serve as architectural accents. You can use the installation steps shown here on a wide variety of outdoor lights.

LAY OUT LIGHTS

BURY THE CABLE

HOOK UP THE TRANSFORMER

INSTALL THE FIXTURES

✳ WHAT'S DIFFERENT?

Low-voltage landscape fixtures accept a wide variety of lightbulbs. The bulb is sometimes included, but buy a few extra bulbs, in case of breakage. Shown below are six popular bulbs used in landscape lighting. Top row: 14-watt flood lamp and MR11 halogen. Bottom row: wedge-base, bi-pin halogen, bayonet-base, and fuse-type.

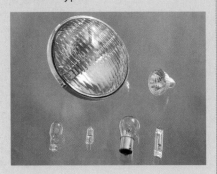

▶ DO IT RIGHT

When installing a landscape lighting system, keep the following rules in mind:

• Place the first light at least 10 ft. away from the transformer.

• Plug the transformer directly into a GFCI-protected outlet; never use an extension cord.

• Keep lights at least 5 ft. away from a swimming pool or pond.

Tools & Gear

To install a landscape lighting system, you'll need a couple of tools that you'd never use for any other lighting project.

FLAT-BLADE SHOVEL. This type of shovel does a good job of digging the narrow trench for burying the cable.

WIRE STRIPPERS. You'll need these to cut and strip insulation from low-voltage cable.

HAND SLEDGE. For this project, we mounted the plug-in transformer on a pressure-treated 2x6 stake that we pounded into the ground beside an outdoor electrical outlet. A 3-lb. hand sledge will help you pound in the 24-in.-long, stake. The sledge and stake aren't needed if you decide to screw the transformer directly to the house.

TAPE MEASURE. Get a 25-ft. or 30-ft. tape to determine the spacing between light fixtures.

PHILLIPS SCREWDRIVER. Use this to tighten the screw terminals when attaching the cable to the transformer.

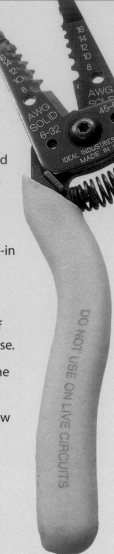

COOL TOOL

A bucket organizer is a great way to keep tools neatly organized and within easy reach. Made of tough-wearing nylon, the organizer fits into any 5-gal. plastic bucket. The model shown here has 35 different pouches, pockets, straps, and sheaths for holding a variety of hand tools and accessories.

Shopping Tips

When shopping for a low-voltage landscape lighting system, you'll discover dozens of different fixtures and accessories in many styles and finishes. However, nearly every system, regardless of how elaborate, is composed of four basic parts:

1 | TRANSFORMER. The power behind every low-voltage system is the transformer. It plugs into a cover-protected outdoor outlet and steps down the house current from 120 volts to 12 volts. Most transformers are equipped with a 24-hour timer that allows you to determine when the lights automatically go on and off. Transformers are rated according to maximum wattage output. Models range from 44 watts to 900 watts. To determine which size transformer you need, add up the wattage of all the lights in the system.

2 | LOW-VOLTAGE ELECTRICAL CABLE. The cable used for landscape lighting is made for burial underground. It runs from the transformer to each light fixture (see the illustration at right). Low-voltage cable is available in 12, 14, and 16 gauge. The lower the number, the thicker the wire and the greater its capacity. Which cable to choose depends largely on the size of the transformer and the length of the cable. For example, a 300-watt transformer can power 100 ft. of 16-gauge cable, 150 ft. of 14-gauge cable, or 200 ft. of 12-gauge cable. Check with the salesperson or manufacturer for cable recommendations for your specific system.

3 | PATHWAY LIGHTS. Designed for installation along a walkway or driveway, this type of fixture represents the most stylish and elegant of all the landscape lights. For this project, the homeowner chose a polished-copper tier light made by Intermatic.

4 | ACCENT FIXTURES. The unsung heroes of any landscape lighting design are the accent lights. These specialty fixtures, which are often hidden from view, include floodlights, spotlights, up-lights, and wall-wash fixtures. They're used to illuminate trees, walls, fences and other landscape features.

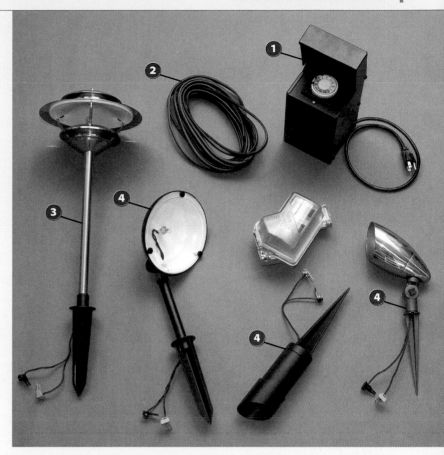

COMPONENTS & CONNECTIONS

Wall-wash fixtures

Stonewall

Low-voltage cable

Outlet transformer

Pathway fixtures

Tree

Outlet transformer

Shrub up-light

Flood light

Laying the Cable

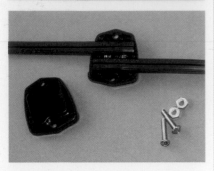

1 **SPACE THE FIXTURES.** Start by carefully unpacking and assembling each light fixture. Screw the shaft (or stem) into the head of the fixture. Then screw the ground stake onto the lower end of the shaft. Install the lightbulb. Lay the fixtures along the pathway, spacing them about 8 ft. to 10 ft. apart. Here, we installed lights along both sides of the path, but in most cases, one line of fixtures provides plenty of illumination.

2 **LAY OUT THE CABLE.** Unroll the spool of low-voltage electrical cable and lay it alongside the path, following the line of light fixtures. If you come to an obstacle, such as a fence or tree, string the cable under or around it. Continue laying the cable all the way to the nearest outdoor electrical outlet.

3 **CUT THE TRENCH.** Use a straight-blade shovel to cut a 2-in.- to 3-in.-deep trench along the line of light fixtures. Position the trench about 5 in. away from the edge of the path. The trench doesn't have to be perfectly straight, so if you hit a rock or root, go around it.

4 **BURY THE CABLE.** Lay the cable into the trench and then shove it down into the ground with a homemade push stick made from a short piece of ½-in. plywood. Don't use the shovel or any other sharp tool to press in the cable; you might slice open the cable's rubber insulation.

1

2

3

4

Installing the Transformer

5 **STRIP OFF THE INSULATION.** Low-voltage cable consists of two bundles of stranded-copper wire. Before you can connect the cable to the transformer, you must peel apart the two bundles. Grab the end of the cable with your finger and peel it down the center to form two 4-in.-long insulated wires. Use wire strippers to remove at least ⅝ in. of insulation from the end of each wire.

6 **CONNECT THE CABLE TO THE TRANSFORMER.** Slide the cable through the white retaining strap on the bottom of the transformer. Insert one wire under the "A" screw terminal, and the other wire under the "B" terminal. Use a Phillips screwdriver to tighten the screws and securely lock the wires in place.

7 **DRIVE IN THE WOOD STAKE.** Next, use a small hand sledge to pound a pressure-treated 2x6 stake into the ground right beside the outdoor electrical outlet. Then, drive two 1¼-in.-long galvanized decking screws into the stake, but don't drive them all the way in. Leave the heads sticking out about ¼ in. Space the screws exactly 3⅞ in. apart.

8 **MOUNT THE TRANSFORMER.** On the back of the transformer are two keyhole slots. Align the slots with the screws sticking out of the stake. Push the transformer onto the screws, then press down to lock the screw heads into the slots. Now use cable staples to secure the low-voltage cable to the stake.

5

6

7

8

Connect the Lights

9   **ATTACH AN ALL-WEATHER COVER.** Remove the spring-loaded weatherproof cover from the outdoor outlet and replace it with a "while-in-use" cover. This oversized plastic box provides extra protection for the outlet and the transformer's power cord. After screwing the while-in-use cover in place, snap on the interior cover plate.

10   **PLUG IN THE TRANSFORMER.** Plug the transformer's power cord into the outlet. Again, be sure that it's a GFCI (ground-fault circuit interrupter) outlet. If it isn't, hire a licensed electrician to install one. Now, swing open the door on top of the transformer and set  the 24-hour timer for whichever times you want the lights to come on and go off.

 **11**   **CONNECT THE FIXTURES.** Here's the fun part of the project: hooking up the lights. Hanging from the bottom of each fixture are two wires. At the end of each wire is a snap-together connector. Slip the two connectors around the small loop of cable protruding from the trench, then pinch them together. Sharp prongs inside of the connectors will pierce the cable and make contact with the wires. Since the transformer is already plugged in, the fixture should light up. If it doesn't, pull apart the connectors and try again or check the bulb.

12   **INSTALL THE LIGHTS.** Stand up the fixture, making sure that it's not on top of the cable, and use two hands to press it into the ground. The round collar at the top of the stake should be flush with the soil. Stand back to see if the fixture is straight and not tilted to one side. If it needs to be straightened up, don't pull on the shaft; you might bend it. Instead, place the tip of the shovel against the stake and use your foot to apply gentle pressure until the fixture is straight.

9 | 10

11 | 12

Doubling as a garden sculpture, this unique two-tulip fixture features a pair of 24-watt lights, a Tiffany-glass butterfly, realistic-looking plant leaves, and a verde finish.

If variety is important, you'll love all the choices you have with landscape lighting. There are numerous low-voltage fixtures, solar-powered lights, and line-voltage systems that run off of 120-volt house current. Choosing the right fixtures for your home can be challenging. To help simplify the selection, keep in mind that landscape lights fall into two basic categories: decorative pathway lights and accent lights, such as floodlights and spotlights.

Here you'll find several fixtures in a wide array of styles and finishes, including weathered copper, pewter, bronze, and rustic-brick brown. For additional help in choosing a landscape lighting system, contact a professional lighting consultant or landscape architect.

Designed to fit discreetly into any garden, this cast-aluminum pathway fixture has a mushroom-cap shade, verde finish, and decorative reeds that resemble plant stems.

A string of attractive Mission-style lights brightens up a set of stone stairs without glare.

Here's a modern version of a traditional pagoda-style lantern. This 37-in.-tall, line-voltage fixture has a white-glass diffuser that radiates a soft glow while reducing glare.

This versatile dual-lamp fixture is fitted with two aluminum shrouds, which you can rotate to direct the light down, up, forward, or back.

Add a little style—and illumination—to a deck railing with this low-voltage, Mission-style post lantern.

This compact, low-voltage fixture provides an inconspicuous way to add accent lighting to a deck. The 3-in.-wide light fits into a notch cut in the underside of the handrail.

Liven up your landscape lighting system—especially around the holidays—with colored bulbs. They're available in amber, blue, green, and red.

Hide a light in plain sight with this low-voltage rock fixture, which is made from a chunk of real granite.

Highlight bushes, small trees, and narrow columns with this 20-watt shrub up-light.

Resembling part of a 1959 Cadillac, this stylish 20-watt floodlight has a highly polished copper finish.

Wall-wash fixtures produce a wide beam of light, which is ideal for illuminating broad, vertical surfaces, and wide stairs.

SOLAR-POWERED FIXTURES

No wiring needed with these solar-powered fixtures. Each one has a photocell and rechargeable battery. Once fully charged, they'll stay lit for up to 15 hours.

Resembling a traditional carriage lantern, this attractive solar-powered fixture has a classic pewter finish.

Above: This straight-shaft lantern has a rustic-brick finish and amber-tinted light. And it doesn't come on until the sun goes down.

These 7½-in.-dia. floating lights provide a safe and easy way to add accent lighting to a pond or pool.

Enliven a flower garden or pond with these solar-powered creatures.

Photo Credits

All photos appearing in this book are © Geoffrey Gross, except:

p. 6: (left) Photos provided by Progress Lighting. For more information, call 1-864-599-6000 or visit www.progresslighting.com

p. 32: (left) © Grey Crawford; (top) © Shades of Light

p. 33: (left) © Randy O'Rourke; (right) Photos provided by Progress Lighting. For more information, call 1-864-599-6000 or visit www.progresslighting.com

p. 34: (left) © Lamps Plus; (right) © Shades of Light

p. 35: (top left) by Roe A. Osborne, courtesy *Fine Homebuilding*, © The Taunton Press, Inc.; (bottom left) Studio Steel, Inc.; (top right) © Lamps Plus; (bottom right) Photos provided by Progress Lighting. For more information, call 1-864-599-6000 or visit www.progresslighting.com

p. 44: (left, top & bottom) © davidduncanlivingston.com; (right, top and bottom) © Geoffrey Gross

p. 45: by Charles Miller, courtesy *Fine Homebuilding*, © The Taunton Press, Inc.

p. 46v (top left) © davidduncanlivingston.com; (bottom left) Photos provided by Progress Lighting. For more information, call 1-864-599-6000 or visit www.progresslighting.com; (right) by Kevin Ireton, courtesy *Fine Homebuilding*, © The Taunton Press, Inc.

p. 47: (top) © davidduncanlivingston.com; (bottom) Courtesy of Sea Gull Lighting Products, Inc.; (right) by Charles Miller, courtesy *Fine Homebuilding*, © The Taunton Press, Inc.

p. 49: © Randy O'Rourke

p. 58: (top left) Photos provided by Progress Lighting. For more information, call 1-864-599-6000 or visit www.progresslighting.com; (bottom left) © Chipper Hatter; (right) © Randy O'Rourke

p. 59: (top) © Ken Gutmaker; (all bottom photos) Photos provided by Progress Lighting. For more information, call 1-864-599-6000 or visit www.progresslighting.com

p. 60: (top left) Photos provided by Progress Lighting. For more information, call 1-864-599-6000 or visit www.progresslighting.com; (bottom left) by Andy Engel, courtesy *Fine Homebuilding*, © The Taunton Press, Inc.; (right) by Charles Miller, courtesy *Fine Homebuilding*, © The Taunton Press, Inc.

p. 61: (top left) © Randy O'Rourke; (bottom left) by Charles Bickford, courtesy *Fine Homebuilding*, © The Taunton Press, Inc.

p. 72: (left, top and bottom) Photos provided by Progress Lighting. For more information, call 1-864-599-6000 or visit www.progresslighting.com; (right) © Randy O'Rourke

p. 73: (left) © Randy O'Rourke; (right, top & bottom) © Geoffrey Gross

p. 74: (left and right) by Charles Bickford, courtesy *Fine Homebuilding*, © The Taunton Press, Inc.

p. 75: (top) by Charles Miller, courtesy *Fine Homebuilding*, © The Taunton Press, Inc.; (bottom) Custom window treatments and home decor provided by Smith + Noble, 800-765-7776; (right) ALKCO Lighting

p. 77: © Randy O'Rourke

p. 79: (bottom) Courtesy of Sea Gull Lighting Products, Inc.

p. 88: (left, top and bottom) Photos provided by Progress Lighting. For more information, call 1-864-599-6000 or visit www.progresslighting.com; (right) © Brian Vanden Brink

p. 89: (left) © davidduncanlivingston.com; (right, top and bottom) © Geoffrey Gross

p. 90: (left and center top & bottom) Photos provided by Progress Lighting. For more information, call 1-864-599-6000 or visit www.progresslighting.com; (right) Courtesy of Sea Gull Lighting Products, Inc.

p. 91: (top and bottom) © davidduncanlivingston.com

p. 93: © Grey Crawford

p. 102: (left) © davidduncanlivingston.com; (right) © Hunter-Kenroy Lighting

For more great weekend project ideas look for these and other
TAUNTON PRESS BOOKS wherever books are sold.

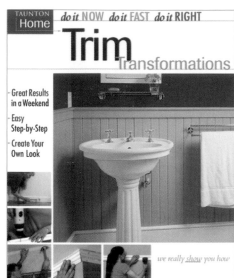

Paint Transformations
1-56158-670-6
Product #070751
$14.95

Trim Transformations
1-56158-671-4
Product #070752
$14.95

Storage Solutions
1-56158-668-4
Product #070754
$14.95

For more information visit our Web site at www.doitnowfastright.com